# NorthStar

## READING AND WRITING

### Basic/Low Intermediate

SECOND EDITION

**Natasha Haugnes**
**Beth Maher**

Series Editors
**Frances Boyd**
**Carol Numrich**

Longman

**NorthStar: Reading and Writing, Basic/Low Intermediate, Second Edition**
Copyright © 2004, 1998 by Pearson Education, Inc.

Pearson Education, 10 Bank Street, White Plains, NY 10606

Development director: Penny Laporte
Project manager: Debbie Sistino
Senior development editor: Françoise Leffler
Vice president, director of design and production: Rhea Banker
Executive managing editor: Linda Moser
Production coordinator: Melissa Leyva
Senior production editor: Kathleen Silloway
Production editor: Andrea C. Basora
Director of manufacturing: Patrice Fraccio
Senior manufacturing buyer: Dave Dickey
Photo research: Aerin Csigay
Cover design: Rhea Banker
Cover art: Detail of Der Rhein bei Duisburg, 1937, 145(R 5) Rhine near
    Duisburg 19 x 27.5 cm; water-based on cardboard; The Metropolitan
    Museum of Art, N.Y. The Berggruen Klee Collection, 1984.
    (1984.315.56) Photograph © 1985 The Metropolitan Museum of Art.
    © 2003 Artists Rights Society (ARS), New York / VG Bild-Kunst, Bonn
Text design: Quorum Creative Services
Text composition: ElectraGraphics, Inc.
Text font: 11/13 Sabon
Illustration credits: see p. 205
Photo credits: see p. 205

**Der Rhein bei Duisburg**
**Paul Klee**

**Library of Congress Cataloging-in-Publication Data**

Haugnes, Natasha
    NorthStar. Reading and writing, basic/low intermediate / Natasha
Haugnes, Beth Maher.
        p. cm.
    Includes index.
        1. English language—Textbooks for foreign speakers. 2. Reading
comprehension—Problems, exercises, etc. 3. Report writing—
Problems, exercises, etc. I. Title: Reading and writing, basic/low
intermediate. II. Maher, Beth III. Title.

PE1128.H394 2003
428.2'4—dc21

2003047517

ISBN:  0-201-75569-6 (Student Book)
       0-13-184671-X (Student Book with CD)

Printed in the United States of America
10—CRK—09 08 07
7 8 9 10—CRK—09 08 07

# Contents

# Welcome to NORTHSTAR

## Second Edition

**NorthStar** leads the way in integrated skills series. The Second Edition remains an innovative, five-level series written for students with academic as well as personal language goals. Each unit of the thematically linked Reading and Writing strand and Listening and Speaking strand explores intellectually challenging, contemporary themes to stimulate critical thinking skills while building language competence.

Four easy to follow sections—Focus on the Topic, Focus on Reading/Focus on Listening, Focus on Vocabulary, and Focus on Writing/Focus on Speaking—invite students to focus on the process of learning through **NorthStar**.

## Thematically Based Units

**NorthStar** engages students by organizing language study thematically. Themes provide stimulating topics for reading, writing, listening, and speaking.

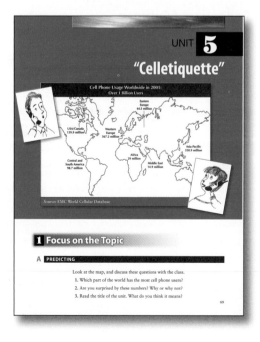

# Extensive Support to Build Skills for Academic Success

Creative activities help students develop language-learning strategies, such as predicting and identifying main ideas and details.

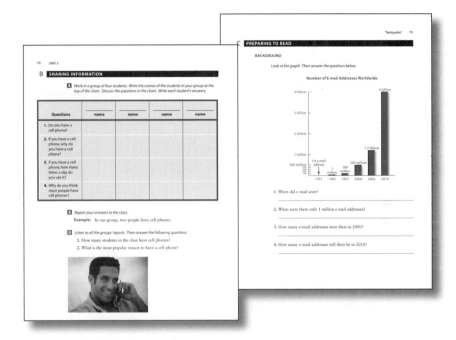

# High-Interest Listening and Reading Selections

The two listening or reading selections in each unit present contrasting viewpoints to enrich students' understanding of the content while building language skills.

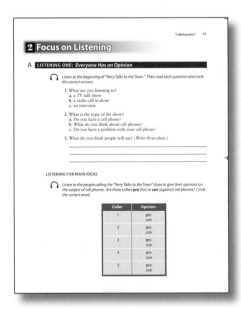

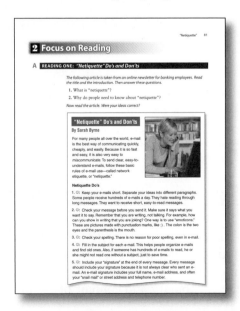

# Critical Thinking Skill Development

Critical thinking skills, such as synthesizing information or reacting to the different viewpoints in the two reading or listening selections, are practiced throughout each unit, making language learning meaningful.

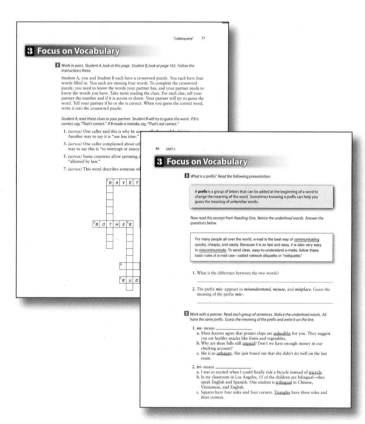

# Extensive Vocabulary Practice

Students are introduced to key, contextualized vocabulary to help them comprehend the listening and reading selections. They also learn idioms, collocations, and word forms to help them explore, review, play with, and expand their spoken and written expression.

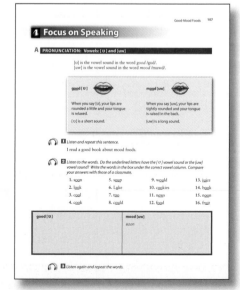

# Powerful Pronunciation Practice

A carefully designed pronunciation syllabus in the Listening and Speaking strand focuses on topics such as stress, rhythm, and intonation. Theme-based pronunciation practice reinforces the vocabulary and content of the unit.

# Content-Rich Grammar Practice

Each thematic unit integrates the study of grammar with related vocabulary and cultural information. The grammatical structures are drawn from the listening or reading selections and offer an opportunity for students to develop accuracy in speaking or writing about the topic.

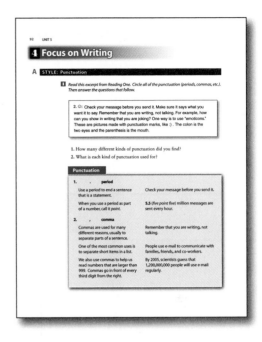

# Extensive Opportunity for Discussion and Writing

Challenging and imaginative speaking activities, writing topics, and research assignments allow students to apply the language, grammar, style, and content they've learned.

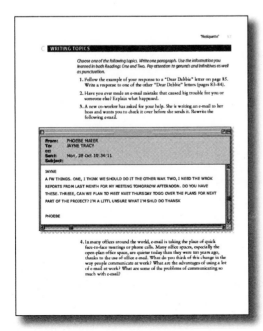

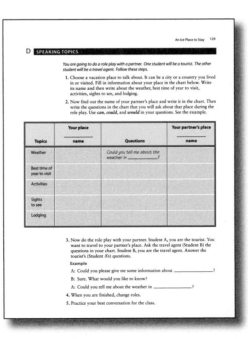

# Writing Activity Book

The companion *Writing Activity Book* leads students through the writing process with engaging writing assignments. Skills and vocabulary from **NorthStar: Reading and Writing,** are reviewed and expanded as students learn the process of prewriting, organizing, revising, and editing.

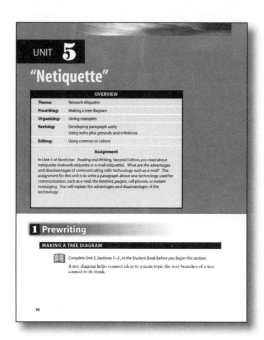

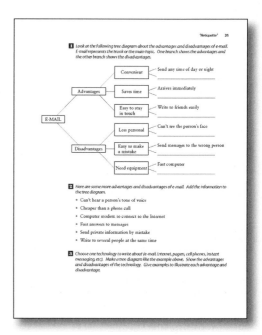

# Audio Program

All the pronunciation, listening, and reading selections have been professionally recorded. The audio program includes audio CDs as well as audio cassettes.

# Teacher's Manual with Achievement Tests

Each book in the series has an accompanying *Teacher's Manual* with step-by-step teaching suggestions, time guidelines, and expansion activities. Also included in each *Teacher's Manual* are reproducible unit-by-unit tests. The Listening and Speaking strand tests are recorded on CD and included in the *Teacher's Manual*. Packaged with each *Teacher's Manual* for the Reading and Writing strand is a TestGen CD-ROM that allows teachers to create and customize their own **NorthStar** tests. Answer Keys to both the Student Book and the Tests are included, along with a unit-by-unit word list of key vocabulary.

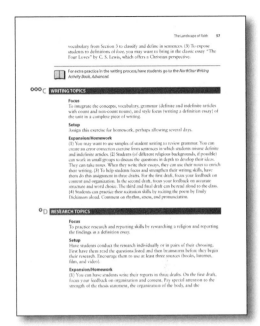

# NorthStar Video Series

Engaging, authentic video clips, including cartoons, documentaries, interviews, and biographies correlate to the themes in **NorthStar.** There are four videos, one for each level of **NorthStar,** Second edition, containing 3- to 5- minute segments for each unit. Worksheets for the video can be found on the **NorthStar** Companion Website.

# Companion Website

**http://www.longman.com/northstar** includes resources for students and teachers such as additional vocabulary activities, Web-based links and research, video worksheets, and correlations to state standards.

# Scope and Sequence

| Unit | Critical Thinking Skills | Reading Tasks |
|---|---|---|
| **1**<br>**Finding the Ideal Job**<br>Theme: Work<br>Reading One: *Finding the Ideal Job*<br>  A review of a job hunter's manual<br>Reading Two: *The Ideal Job*<br>  A newspaper report | Interpret a cartoon<br>Recognize personal attitudes and preferences<br>Classify information<br>Evaluate information according to criteria set forth in a text<br>Infer information not explicit in the text<br>Hypothesize another's point of view | Read a bar graph<br>Make predictions<br>Read for main ideas<br>Scan for details<br>Relate personal experience to the text<br>Connect concepts between two texts |
| **2**<br>**Country Life vs. City Life**<br>Theme: The Country and the City<br>Reading One: *The Farming Life for Me*<br>  A letter to the editor<br>Reading Two: *Leaving the Farm*<br>  A newspaper report | Compare family histories<br>Interpret statistics<br>Infer information not explicit in the text<br>Support answers with information from the text<br>Hypothesize another's point of view<br>Classify information<br>Evaluate advantages and disadvantages<br>Compare and contrast city and country life | Make predictions<br>Identify main ideas<br>Identify supporting information<br>Locate passages in the text<br>Scan for details<br>React to the reading with personal opinions<br>Synthesize information from two texts |
| **3**<br>**Making Money**<br>Theme: Money<br>Reading One: *Making Money*<br>  A magazine article<br>Reading Two: *I Made It Myself*<br>  A counterfeiter's account | Identify personal values and assumptions<br>Infer word meaning from context<br>Infer information not explicit in text<br>Support answers with information from the text<br>Draw logical conclusions<br>Compare and contrast types of money and types of counterfeiters | Make predictions<br>Identify main ideas<br>Search for and locate details<br>Relate previous knowledge to information in the text<br>Understand pronouns<br>Synthesize information from two texts |
| **4**<br>**Save the Elephants**<br>Theme: Animals<br>Reading One: *Save the Elephants*<br>  A fundraising appeal<br>Reading Two: *Save a Logger—Eat an Owl*<br>  A letter to the editor | Classify information<br>Recognize personal assumptions and values<br>Infer word meaning from context<br>Identify cause and effect<br>Support personal opinions with information from the text | Make predictions<br>Identify main ideas<br>Scan for information<br>Identify the purpose and audience of a text<br>Identify connecting themes between two texts<br>Research an endangered animal |
| **5**<br>**"Netiquette"**<br>Theme: Network Etiquette<br>Reading One: *"Netiquette" Do's and Don'ts*<br>  An excerpt from an online newsletter<br>Reading Two: *Dear Debbie*<br>  A newspaper advice column | Interpret a cartoon<br>Interpret a bar graph<br>Compare personal use of e-mail<br>Infer word meaning from context<br>Evaluate situations according to criteria set forth in a text<br>Identify the advantages and disadvantages of e-mail | Make predictions<br>Summarize a text<br>Identify supporting ideas in a text<br>Connect concepts between two texts<br>Research e-mail etiquette |

| Writing Tasks | Vocabulary | Grammar |
| --- | --- | --- |
| Construct complete sentences<br>Edit incomplete or incorrect sentences<br>Compose a paragraph response<br>Develop interview questions<br>Summarize an interview<br>Edit and evaluate a classmate's summary | Word definitions<br>Synonyms<br>Vocabulary classification | Descriptive and possessive adjectives |
| Write a paragraph with a topic sentence, supporting sentences, and a concluding sentence<br>Develop topic sentences<br>Arrange a logical paragraph<br>Write a personal letter<br>Write a narrative account in simple past<br>Compose interview questions<br>Edit and evaluate a classmate's paragraph | Word definitions<br>Context clues<br>Multiple definitions | Simple past tense |
| Connect and contrast ideas with transition words<br>Arrange a logical paragraph<br>Write a report using transition words<br>Write sentences of comparison<br>Write a paragraph response<br>Write a business letter<br>Edit and evaluate a classmate's business letter | Context clues<br>Developing word definitions<br>Antonyms | Comparative forms of adjectives |
| Write a cause and effect paragraph<br>Write a personal and a business letter<br>Form correct questions<br>Summarize research in a persuasive letter<br>Edit and evaluate classmates' persuasive letters | Word definitions<br>Context clues<br>Vocabulary classification | *Wh-* questions in the simple present tense |
| Practice correct use of punctuation<br>Edit punctuation usage in a passage<br>Write a letter of advice<br>Compose an e-mail reply<br>Write a paragraph response<br>Summarize research in a paragraph<br>Edit and evaluate a classmate's summary | Word definitions<br>Context clues<br>Prefixes | Verbs plus gerunds and infinitives |

| Unit | Critical Thinking Skills | Reading Tasks |
|------|--------------------------|---------------|
| **6**<br><br>**Women's Work?**<br><br>Theme: Male and Female Roles<br><br>Reading One: *Housework*<br>  A poem<br><br>Reading Two: *Good-bye to (Some) Housework*<br>  A magazine article | Compare past and current family roles<br>Identify point of view in a text<br>Support personal opinion with reasoning<br>Compare past and current gender roles in American families<br>Infer information not explicit in the text<br>Analyze use of rhyme in a poem | Make predictions<br>Read a chart<br>Identify main ideas<br>Locate details in the text<br>Summarize main ideas<br>Synthesize information from two texts<br>Read a questionnaire |
| **7**<br><br>**Organic Produce:  Is It Worth the Price?**<br><br>Theme: Food<br><br>Reading One: *Organic Produce vs. Regular Produce*<br>  A newspaper advice column<br><br>Reading Two: *What's in Our Food?*<br>  Food labels | Establish criteria for choosing produce<br>Evaluate and classify information<br>Infer word meaning from context<br>Hypothesize another's point of view<br>Draw conclusions<br>Deliberate a case using information from the readings<br>Compare and contrast types of produce | Read pricing labels<br>Make predictions<br>Identify main ideas<br>Scan for details<br>Relate personal values to information in a text<br>Synthesize information in two texts<br>Read a recipe |
| **8**<br><br>**"I'll take the train, thanks."**<br><br>Theme: Travel<br><br>Reading One: *The Climate Train*<br>  A magazine article<br><br>Reading Two: *On the Road with John Madden*<br>  A newspaper report | Evaluate best method of travel<br>Infer word meaning from context<br>Infer information not explicit in the text<br>Hypothesize another's point of view<br>Interpret people's motivations and values<br>Correlate specific examples to broad categories | Read a map<br>Make predictions<br>Identify main ideas<br>Scan for information in the text<br>Link information from two texts using a graphic organizer<br>Relate life experiences to texts |
| **9**<br><br>**The Winter Blues**<br><br>Theme: Health and Illness<br><br>Reading One: *Seasonal Affective Disorder*<br>  An excerpt from a medical guide<br><br>Reading Two: *A SAD Woman in Alaska*<br>  A case study | Interpret a picture<br>Compare and contrast definitions<br>Infer word meaning from context<br>Classify information from the text<br>Identify advantages and disadvantages of treatments<br>Draw conclusions<br>Deliberate cases using information from the readings | Make predictions<br>Identify main ideas<br>Summarize information in a text using a graphic organizer<br>Read a chart<br>Relate a text to personal experience<br>Research medical depression |
| **10**<br><br>**Endangered Cultures**<br><br>Theme: Endangered Cultures<br><br>Reading One: *Will Indigenous Cultures Survive?*<br>  A magazine article<br><br>Reading Two: *The Penan*<br>  An excerpt from a travelogue | Compare and contrast two images<br>Support inferences with information from a text<br>Contrast different cultural points of view<br>Classify information in the text<br>Hypothesize the future of cultures using information from the readings | Read a map<br>Make predictions<br>Identify main ideas<br>Locate supporting details in a text<br>Draw examples from one text to support broad themes in another<br>Research an endangered culture |

| Writing Tasks | Vocabulary | Grammar |
|---|---|---|
| Compose a rhyming stanza<br>Identify rhyming words<br>Write sentences and questions using adverbs of frequency<br>Compose a questionnaire<br>Write a report on survey results | Context clues<br>Appropriate word usage<br>Vocabulary classification | Adverbs and expressions of frequency |
| Analyze content, tone and intended audience of texts<br>Write a memo<br>Write a persuasive letter<br>Write a recipe<br>Write an explanation<br>Write a produce shopping guide | Context clues<br>Vocabulary classification<br>Word association | Count and non-count nouns |
| Connect sentences with *and* and *but*<br>Write paragraph responses<br>Take notes for research<br>Write a report summarizing data<br>Edit and evaluate a classmate's report | Synonyms<br>Word definitions<br>Context clues | *Can* and *could* |
| Report a conversation using direct speech<br>Edit punctuation in a passage with direct speech<br>Compose an e-mail<br>Write statements of advice<br>Write a paragraph response<br>Write an informational brochure on depression<br>Edit and evaluate a classmate's brochure | Editing words for meaning<br>Context clues | *Should* and *shouldn't* |
| Supply examples to support general statements<br>Form varied questions<br>Write a paragraph response<br>Take notes for research<br>Write a report using research<br>Edit and evaluate a classmate's report | Paraphrase word meaning<br>Context clues<br>Appropriate word usage | Expressing predictions and future plans with the simple future, *be going to,* and the present progressive |

# Acknowledgments

We would like to thank Carol Numrich for her support, insight, and vision. We would also like to thank Françoise Leffler and Debbie Sistino and all those at Pearson Education who worked long and hard to complete this project.

To Beth's sons, Niko and Toby and to her husband, Tom: Thank you for all your love, patience and support throughout this project.

Natasha acknowledges Dr. Pat Porter's wonderful guidance during her days at San Francisco State University. She also extends huge thank yous to John and Emmet for their endless love and understanding.

*Natasha Haugnes* and *Beth Maher*

## Reviewers

For the comments and insights they graciously offered to help shape the direction of the Second Edition of NorthStar, the publisher would like to thank all our reviewers and institutions.

**Lubie G. Alatriste**, Lehman College; **A. Morgan Andaluz**, Leeward Community College; **Chris Antonellis**, Boston University CELOP; **Christine Baez**, Universidad de las Américas, Mexico City, Mexico; **Betty Baron**, Johnson County Community College; **Rudy Besikof**, University of California San Diego; **Mary Black**, Institute of North American Studies; **Dorothy Buroh**, University of California, San Diego; **Kay Caldwell**, Leeward Community College; **Margarita Canales**; Universidad Latinoamericana, Mexico City, Mexico; **Jose Carvalho**, University of Massachusetts Boston; **Philip R. Condorelli**, University of Massachusetts Boston; **Pamela Couch**, Boston University CELOP; **Barbara F. Dingee**, University of Massachusetts Boston; **Jeanne M. Dunnet**, Central Connecticut State University; **Samuela Eckstut-Didier**, Boston University CELOP; **Patricia Hedden**, Yonsei University; **Hostos Community College**; **GEOS Language Institute**; **Jennifer M. Gerrity**, University of Massachusetts Boston; **Lis Jenkinson**, Northern Virginia Community College; **Glenna Jennings**, University of California, San Diego; **Diana Jones**, Instituto Angloamericano, Mexico City, Mexico; **Matt Kaeiser**, Old Dominion University; **Regina Kandraska**, University of Massachusetts Boston; **King Fahd University of Petroleum & Minerals**; **Chris Ko**, Kyang Hee University; **Charalambos Kollias**, The Hellenic-American Union; **Barbara Kruchin**, Columbia University ALP; **Language Training Institute**; **Jacqueline LoConde**, Boston University CELOP; **Mary Lynch**, University of Massachusetts Boston; **Julia Paranionova**, Moscow State Pedagogical University; **Pasadena City College**; **Pontifical Xavier University**; **Natalya Morozova**, Moscow State Pedagogical University; **Mary Carole Ramiowski**, University of Seoul; **Jon Robinson**, University of Seoul; **Michael Sagliano**, Leeward Community College; **Janet Shanks**, Columbia University ALP; **Eric Tejeda**; PROULEX, Guadalajara, Mexico; **Truman College**; **United Arab Emirates University**; **University of Minnesota**; **Karen Whitlow**, Johnson County Community College

# Finding the Ideal Job

## **1** Focus on the Topic

### A  PREDICTING

Look at the cartoon, and discuss these questions with the class.

1. What is the young man doing?

2. What kinds of work is he thinking of?

3. What do you think is the ideal job (the best job) for this young man?

1

## B  SHARING INFORMATION

*Read the statements. How much do you agree or disagree? For each statement, check (✓) the box that shows what you think. Discuss your answers with the class.*

| Statements | Strongly Agree | Agree | Disagree | Strongly Disagree |
|---|---|---|---|---|
| **1.** Enjoying your work is more important than making a lot of money. | | | | |
| **2.** Working with a lot of people is better than working alone. | | | | |
| **3.** Working from home is better than working at an office. | | | | |
| **4.** Working indoors is better than working outdoors. | | | | |

## C  PREPARING TO READ

### BACKGROUND

*Study this graph about job satisfaction (happiness in your job). Then work in a small group, and discuss the questions that follow.*

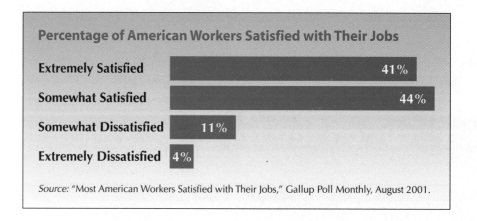

**Percentage of American Workers Satisfied with Their Jobs**

Extremely Satisfied — 41%
Somewhat Satisfied — 44%
Somewhat Dissatisfied — 11%
Extremely Dissatisfied — 4%

*Source:* "Most American Workers Satisfied with Their Jobs," Gallup Poll Monthly, August 2001.

1. Look at the graph. What percentage of Americans have the most job satisfaction? What percentage have the least job satisfaction?

**2.** According to the graph, 85 percent of American workers are *at least* somewhat satisfied with their jobs. Does this number surprise you? Why or why not?

**3.** Think of the people you know in your country who are working. What percentage of them do you think are satisfied with their jobs? What percentage do you think are *not* satisfied?

**4.** What would you do if you felt dissatisfied with your job?

## VOCABULARY FOR COMPREHENSION

*Read the list of words and their definitions. Then complete the sentences with words from the list.*

**career:** the kind of work a person does, usually after learning how and usually for a long time

**employment:** work someone pays you for

**hire:** to give someone a job

**ideal:** perfect

**manager:** the person in charge of a group of workers

**out of work:** without a job

**résumé:** a piece of paper with your work and education history

**rewards:** good things you get in return for work (such as money or health insurance)

**satisfied:** to feel good or happy about something

**skill:** something that you can do well; ability that you have learned and practiced

**want ads:** advertisements, usually in a newspaper, for jobs that are available

**1.** In 1930, jobs were hard to find. Almost 25 percent of all Americans were
_____out of work_____ .

**2.** He's had many different jobs, but only one _____. In other words, he's worked in many different schools, but he's always been a teacher.

**3.** Most companies ask for a(n) _____ so they can read about you before they talk to you in person.

**4.** She sells a lot of her paintings. She has a lot of _____ as an artist and a businesswoman.

5. Let's _____ Katlyn. She has the most experience. She will be a great teacher.

6. She started looking for a job by reading the _____.

7. I worked for weeks on this report. I couldn't seem to get it just right. Yesterday I changed around a few things and added a new section. I think it's good now. Finally, I'm _____ with my work.

8. The _____ of her job just weren't enough. She was happy with the work, but she wasn't making enough money.

9. She was a computer programmer for ten years. Then she became a(n) _____. Suddenly, she had to lead all the people she used to work with.

10. I want to know about your past _____. Where did you work last?

11. Jayne thought Sue was the _____ worker. She was smart, fast, friendly, and very good at her job.

# 2 Focus on Reading

## A  READING ONE: *Finding the Ideal Job*

*Imagine you are not satisfied with your job. You decide to job hunt—that is, to look for a new job. With a partner, write a list of things you might do to find a job.*

1. *I might ask someone in my family for a job.* _____

2. _____

3. _____

4. _____

5. _____

*Now learn what a professional has to say about this topic.  Read a book review of a job-hunting manual.*

## *The Book Review*

# FINDING THE IDEAL JOB

*What Color Is Your Parachute?: A Practical Manual for Job Hunters and Career Changers*, by Richard Nelson Bolles, Ten Speed Press, $16.95.

1   You are out of work.
You hate your job.
You aren't satisfied with your career.
You are looking for your first job. Where do you start?

2    If you are like most Americans, you'll probably send your résumé to a lot of companies. You might answer newspaper want ads every Sunday. Or you might go to employment agencies. But experts[1] say you won't have much luck. People find jobs only five to fifteen percent of the time when they use these methods. So, what can you do?

3    One thing you can do is read Richard Bolles's *What Color Is Your Parachute*[2]? Bolles is an expert in the field of job hunting. He has helped thousands of people find jobs and careers. This book is different from other job-hunting manuals. Bolles doesn't help you to find just another job. Instead, he helps you find your ideal job: a job that fits who you are, a job that is satisfying to you. What kind of job is ideal for you? If you don't know the answer, Bolles says, you can't find your ideal job. You need to have a clear picture in your mind of the job you want. The book has many exercises to help you draw this picture.

4    Bolles says that you must think about three things:
    (1) **Your skills.** What do you like to do? What do you do well? Do you like talking? Helping people? Teaching? Reading and writing? Using computers? Working with your hands? Bolles asks you to think about all your skills, not only "work skills." For example, a mother of four children is probably good at managing people (children!). She may be a good manager.
    (2) **Job setting.** Where do you like to work? Do you like to work outside? At home? In an office? Alone or with others? What kind of people do you like to work with?
    (3) **Job rewards.** How much money do you need? How much money do you want? What else do you want from a job? What would make you feel good about a job?

[1] *expert:* a person who knows a lot about something.
[2] *parachute:* something you wear when you jump out of a plane. When you jump, it opens up and it stops you from hitting the ground very hard.

5    After Bolles helps you decide on your ideal job, he gives you specific advice on how to find the job. His exercises teach you how to find companies and how to introduce yourself. The chapter on job interviews is full of useful information and suggestions. For example, most people go to interviews asking themselves the question, "How do I get the company to hire me?" Bolles thinks this is the wrong question. Instead, he wants you to ask yourself, "Do I really want to work for this company?"

6    There are two small problems with the book. First, Bolles writes too much! He explains some of his ideas over and over again. Second, there is no space to write the answers to the exercises. But these are small problems. *What Color Is Your Parachute?* is the best job-hunting manual available today.

7    *What Color Is Your Parachute?* was written in 1970. But the information is updated[3] every year. So, if you are looking for a job, or if you have a job but want a new one, remember: Don't just send out copies of your résumé. Don't just answer want ads. And don't wait for friends to get you a job. Instead, buy this book and do a job hunt the right way.

*Barbara Kleppinger*

[3] **updated:** changed to reflect new information.

## READING FOR MAIN IDEAS

*Read each statement. Decide if it is true or false. Write **T** (true) or **F** (false) next to it. Compare your answers with a classmate's.*

_____  **1.** *What Color Is Your Parachute?* is similar to other job-hunting manuals.

_____  **2.** Bolles's goal is to help people find jobs as quickly as possible.

_____  **3.** According to *What Color Is Your Parachute?*, job hunters should think about their skills, the job setting, and the job rewards they want.

_____  **4.** *What Color Is Your Parachute?* includes specific advice on finding jobs.

_____  **5.** According to the reviewer, the book is too short.

## READING FOR DETAILS

*Write each job-hunting method listed below in the correct column in the chart on page 7.*

answer newspaper want ads
ask friends to help
decide what kind of job is ideal
think about job rewards
do exercises

go to an employment agency
decide what kind of place you
   want to work in
send out lots of résumés
think about your skills

| What Many People Do to Find a Job | What Bolles Says Will Help You Find a Job |
| --- | --- |
| *answer newspaper want ads* | |

## REACTING TO THE READING

**1** *Read each situation. Decide whether, according to Bolles, the person is making a mistake or doing the right thing. Circle your answer. Then discuss your decisions with the class.*

1. Owen was always a manager. He doesn't want to be a manager. But he's not looking for another job because he thinks that he doesn't know how to do anything else. According to Bolles, Owen is _____.

   **a.** making a mistake
   **b.** doing the right thing

2. Amy studied to be a teacher. But now she's not just looking for work as a teacher. Instead, she's thinking about whether teaching is really the right career for her. According to Bolles, Amy is _____.

   **a.** making a mistake
   **b.** doing the right thing

3. Bill is in a job interview. He is asking the person who is interviewing him some questions about the company. According to Bolles, Bill is _____.

   **a.** making a mistake
   **b.** doing the right thing

4. Kathy has a choice between a job that pays very well and a job that seems very interesting. She decides that for her, money is the most important thing. So she chooses the job that pays well. According to Bolles, Kathy is _____.

   **a.** making a mistake
   **b.** doing the right thing

5. Peter sent his résumé to many companies and he answered many want ads. So now he is waiting for someone to call him about a job. According to Bolles, Peter is _____.

   **a.** making a mistake
   **b.** doing the right thing

**2** *Discuss the following questions with a partner. Give your opinions. Share your ideas with the class.*

1. The next time you look for a job, which of Bolles's ideas do you think you might use?

2. You are in an interview for a job with a very interesting company. What questions might you ask the interviewer about this company?

3. The title of the book is *What Color Is Your Parachute?* Why do you think the author chose this title?

---

**B    READING TWO:  *The Ideal Job***

*Read these stories about people who love their jobs.*

# THE IDEAL JOB

## BY ALEX FROST

1   Believe it or not, some people get paid—and well—for doing the things that make them really happy. Here are a few people who have found the job of their dreams.

**"I know all about job-hunting."—Betsy**

2   A few years ago, I lost my job as a manager in a factory. I was so unhappy. I was 38 years old, out of work for the 100th time, and without much hope. Then, one day I was thinking about the question, "What do I do best?" and the answer came to me. I had been out of work many times, so I knew every manual about how to find a job or change a career. I must have been to over 100 interviews in my life, made 1,000 phone calls asking for jobs, and sent out a résumé to almost 2,000 companies. When I looked at my skills, I saw that my best skills were job-hunting skills! So I started my own company, Career Consulting. It's a business that helps people find jobs. I hired two people to work with me. The three of us work together on everything, but I'm the boss. It's great. I love the work, and I make a lot of money!

**"I have the funnest job in the world."
—Amanda**

3    I have been a matchmaker for 41 years. Because of me, 60 couples are now happily married or engaged. I'm a good matchmaker. I have a very good eye for people. And I don't mean I match people on how they look. I mean, I can meet a person just once for ten minutes, and I know for sure what kind of person he or she is. I get a feeling. And this feeling tells me, "Oh, he would be a great husband for Stephanie," or "Ah, now here is the woman for Timothy." I can't imagine a job that's more fun. I meet wonderful people. I work for myself. Nobody tells me what to do. I make enough money to live a simple life. And I get so much joy from seeing what happens to my matches. A month ago a couple stopped by on their way home from the hospital with their new baby girl. I'm so happy to think that I helped make that family!

**"I have a job with an incredible view."—
Donna**

4    Teaching skydiving[1] is so exciting. I love seeing students on their first jump. They are all nervous and excited. When they get to the ground, they can't wait to call everyone they know and tell them they just jumped out of an airplane. Later, when they learn to turn and fly forward, they realize that they're not just a flying stone. They realize that they're like a bird—they can fly!

5    It wasn't easy to get this job. I had to have about 1,000 jumps and about two years of training. And the salary was only $15,000 for the first year. But I don't do it for the money. In fact, I don't need to get paid at all. I love it that much!

---

[1] *skydiving:* the sport of jumping out of airplanes with a parachute.

*Source:* Based on information in Dave Curtin, "From Sky Diving Instructors to Fashion Consultants, Some Folks Just Love Their Jobs," Knight-Ridder/Tribune News Service, 11 March 1996.

---

*Complete the sentences with the correct name from the reading.*

1. _____*Donna*_____ made $15,000 her first year.

2. _____ helped 60 couples find each other.

3. _____ was out of work many times.

4. _____ has had the same job for over 40 years.

5. _____ changed careers.

6. _____ loves teaching.

## C  LINKING READINGS ONE AND TWO

*Look at Reading One again. Reread the paragraphs about skills, setting, and rewards. How would the women in Reading Two answer the questions in these paragraphs? Write answers for each woman.*

1. **Betsy**

   Skills: *I have a lot of job-hunting skills.*

   Setting: _____

   Rewards: _____

2. **Amanda**

   Skills: _____

   Setting: _____

   Rewards: _____

3. **Donna**

   Skills: _____

   Setting: _____

   Rewards: _____

4. **What about you? How do you answer these questions?**

   Your name: _____

   Skills: _____

   Setting: _____

   Rewards: _____

# 3 Focus on Vocabulary

**1** *Cross out the word or phrase that is not related to the boldfaced word(s).*

1. **résumé:** work history, job hunting, ~~money~~

2. **want ad:** newspaper, skill, job

3. **salary:** vacation, money, job

4. **employment agency:** secretary, job hunt, résumé

5. **career:** city, work, experience

6. **out of work:** job hunting, manager, free time

7. **manual:** book, information, newspaper

8. **boss:** owner, manager, job hunter

9. **factory:** fact, company, business

10. **training:** school, career, learning

**2** *Complete the e-mail from Cristina to Jenny with words from the list.*

| career | hire | out of work | ideal | résumé | skills | manager |
|---|---|---|---|---|---|---|

---

**New Job :)**

**From:** Cristina_Bond@Richmond.edu
**To:** JRIOS@springboard.com
**Sent:** 01 October 2004 14:23
**Subject:** New Job :)

Hi Jenny,

Guess what? I finally found a job. Not just any job. A really great one: Web page designer. I think this might be the (1) _____ job for me. I'm so excited! I thought I was going to be (2) _____ forever.

Remember how I told you that I sent my (3) _____ to about 300 Internet companies? Well, two weeks ago I met this woman on the bus and we started talking, and the next thing you know she's setting up an interview for me with her (4) _____. I was so nervous during the interview. At first he asked me about my last job. I was afraid he wouldn't want to (5) _____ me because I didn't use computers in my last job. But then he started to ask me lots of specific questions about designing Web pages. I'm so glad I took that Web design course last summer. It gave me all the (6) _____ I need to do this job.

Wow, I can't believe it. I'm starting my (7) _____ as a Web page designer. I'll e-mail you next week with my new work number and e-mail address.

Yours,

Web Master[1] Cristina

---

[1] *Web Master:* the job title for people who design Internet web pages.

**3** *Jenny is responding to an e-mail from her friend Cristina. Complete the e-mail. Use the words in parentheses.*

---

**Needing Help**

**From:**  JRIOS@springboard.com
**To:**  Cristina_Bond@Richmond.edu
**Sent:**  3 October 2004 11:16
**Subject:**  Needing help

Hi Cristina,

Glad you finally found a job. Jobs are so difficult to find, or to keep. I just lost my job, and I need to find a new one very soon. Where do I start? Could you help me? I have so many questions:

(résumé)    *Do I need a new résumé?*

(skills)    _____

(salary)    _____

(want ads)_____

(employment agency)_____

(manual)    _____

(boss)    _____

(your idea)_____

Thanks for your help. And best of luck in your new career. Can't wait to hear more about the job!

Love,

Jenny

# 4 Focus on Writing

## A  STYLE:  The Sentence

**1** *Read the following lines. Then answer the questions.*

    **a.** Marika worked for a big camera company for six years.

    **b.** My friend in Boston.

    **c.** He's tired.

    **d.** Teaches mathematics to students at a good college in Massachusetts.

1. Which ones are sentences?

2. Which aren't sentences? How do you know?

### Parts of the Sentence

| | |
|---|---|
| **1.** Every sentence in English must have a subject and a verb. | S   V<br>**She works.** |
| A sentence can have just a subject and a verb.  But, usually, sentences have other words, too. | S   V<br>**She works** for an employment agency. |
| **2.** In commands, we don't say or write a subject.  But the subject of commands is always understood as "you." | V<br>**Answer** the want ads. = *You answer* the want ads. |
| **3.** Subjects come before the verb and often come at the beginning of the sentence. | S   V<br>**Connie** told me it was a great job. |
| **4.** Subjects can be one word or many words. | S<br>**They** told me it was a great job.<br><br>    S<br>**Connie and Jack** told me it was a great job. |
| Subjects can't be repeated. |     S1   S2<br>WRONG: **Connie she** told me it was a great job. |
| **5.** The first letter of the first word of a sentence must be capitalized.<br>A sentence must end with a period, question mark, or exclamation point. | **T**here was one problem.<br><br>I was bored**.** |

**2** *Each sentence has one mistake. Correct the mistakes.*

1. The camera company ~~it~~ paid Marika a lot of money.

2. She happy with her job at the camera company.

3. Decided to change her job anyway.

4. her didn't understand her decision.

5. Why did she change her job

6. Marika she just wanted her dream job.

7. Started Marika her own restaurant.

8. Marika happier now than ever before!

**3** *Read the e-mail below. Like most people, the writer of this e-mail did not always use complete sentences. Underline the incomplete sentences and write them as complete sentences on the lines provided.*

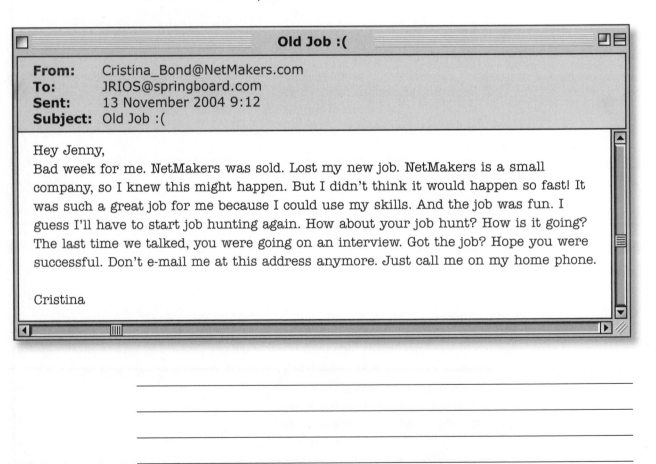

**Old Job :(**

**From:**     Cristina_Bond@NetMakers.com
**To:**       JRIOS@springboard.com
**Sent:**     13 November 2004 9:12
**Subject:**  Old Job :(

Hey Jenny,
Bad week for me. NetMakers was sold. Lost my new job. NetMakers is a small company, so I knew this might happen. But I didn't think it would happen so fast! It was such a great job for me because I could use my skills. And the job was fun. I guess I'll have to start job hunting again. How about your job hunt? How is it going? The last time we talked, you were going on an interview. Got the job? Hope you were successful. Don't e-mail me at this address anymore. Just call me on my home phone.

Cristina

_____

_____

_____

_____

**4** *Write five sentences to describe someone's job—for example, your job, your mother's job, your father's job, or a friend's job.*

**Example**   My friend Jennifer is a kindergarten teacher. Her job is very hard.
She is tired every day. Her job is also a lot of fun. Her job does
not pay a lot of money.

_____

_____

_____

_____

_____

## B   GRAMMAR:  Descriptive Adjectives and Possessive Adjectives

**1** *Read the e-mail again. Notice the underlined words. They are two kinds of adjectives:* ***descriptive adjectives*** *and* ***possessive adjectives.***

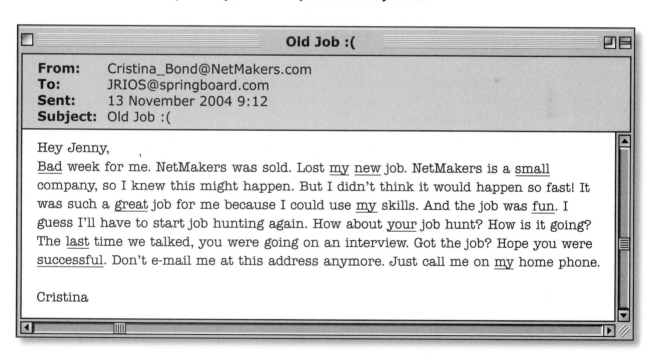

**Old Job :(**

**From:**   Cristina_Bond@NetMakers.com
**To:**   JRIOS@springboard.com
**Sent:**   13 November 2004 9:12
**Subject:**   Old Job :(

Hey Jenny,
<u>Bad</u> week for me. NetMakers was sold. Lost <u>my</u> <u>new</u> job. NetMakers is a <u>small</u> company, so I knew this might happen. But I didn't think it would happen so fast! It was such a <u>great</u> job for me because I could use <u>my</u> skills. And the job was <u>fun</u>. I guess I'll have to start job hunting again. How about <u>your</u> job hunt? How is it going? The <u>last</u> time we talked, you were going on an interview. Got the job? Hope you were <u>successful</u>. Don't e-mail me at this address anymore. Just call me on <u>my</u> home phone.

Cristina

*List each adjective in the e-mail on one of the lines.*

**1.** Descriptive adjectives: _bad,_ _____

**2.** Possessive adjectives: _my,_ _____

## Descriptive and Possessive Adjectives

| | |
|---|---|
| 1. **Descriptive adjectives** describe nouns. They can come after the verb *be*. | She is *smart.* |
| They can come before a noun. | She is a *smart* teacher. |
| When a noun follows an adjective, use *a, an,* or *the* before the adjective. (*A* and *an* are used only with count nouns; see Unit 7.) | She's **a *smart* teacher.** She's **an *important* writer.** **The *new* teacher** isn't here. |
| Remember: Do not use *a, an,* or *the* when the adjective is not followed by a noun. | Gary is *smart.* |
| 2. **Possessive adjectives** show belonging. | I have a job. ***My*** job is very interesting. |
| A noun always follows a possessive adjective. When using possessive adjectives, do not use *a, an,* or *the.* | ***His* boss** is nice. |
| Possessive adjectives have the same form before singular or plural nouns. | ***Your* painting** is beautiful. ***Your* paintings** are beautiful. |

**Possessive Adjectives**

| | | | | |
|---|---|---|---|---|
| *my* | *your* | *his* | *her* | *its* |
| *our* | *your* | *their* | | |

**2** *Use the words to write sentences.*

1. for / Jenny / a / is / career / looking / new    <u>Jenny is looking for a new career.</u>

2. like / She / job / didn't / old / her    _____

3. Our / funny / manager / and / is / smart    _____

4. want ads / job / his / Juan / new / found / in / the    _____

5. sister / out / work / of / is / My    _____

6. an / Richard Bolles / job / interesting / has    _____

**3** *Describe the pictures. For each picture, write at least three sentences. Use at least one possessive adjective, one descriptive adjective before a noun, and one descriptive adjective after* be. *You can use the descriptive adjectives listed below.*

| | | | | | | |
|---|---|---|---|---|---|---|
| big | dirty | hungry | messy | sad | sleepy | young |
| curly | happy | long | old | short | straight | |

**1.** The man:

<u>The man is young. He has short hair. He is hungry.</u>

<u>He drives an old truck.</u>

The truck:

<u>His truck is old. The old truck is dirty.</u>

**2.** The woman:

_____

The desk:

_____

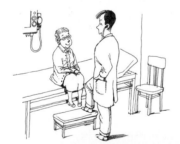

**3.** The doctor:

_____

The patient:

_____

## C   WRITING TOPICS

*Choose one of the following topics. Write one paragraph. Use some of the vocabulary, grammar, and style that you learned in this unit. Be sure to write correct sentences.*

**1.** Imagine your friend just finished college and doesn't know what to do for work. Write him or her a short note with advice. Use information from the review of *What Color Is Your Parachute?* Give at least three suggestions.

**2.** Do you know anyone who has found his or her dream job? Write about this person. Answer these questions: Who is he or she? What does he or she do? How did he or she get the job? What is most important to him or her about the job?

**3.** Imagine you have your dream job. What do you do? Describe your job. Be sure to discuss the three things that Richard Bolles says are important: the skills you use, the setting, and the rewards.

## D  RESEARCH TOPIC

*Work in pairs. Interview someone who wants to change careers. This person might be a classmate, a teacher, a neighbor, or a relative. Follow these steps.*

1. With your partner, prepare a list of questions for your interview. You could start with the following questions and then add some questions of your own to the list.

    a. What is your name?

    b. What is your career now?

    c. What do you do in your career?

    d. What are the good and bad things about your career?

    e. What kind of career do you want to have? Why?

    f. Why would you like this ideal career better than the career you have now?

    g. _____

    h. _____

2. You and your partner interview the person. One of you asks the questions, the other one takes notes.

3. After the interview, you and your partner write a report. Describe the job that person has and the job that he or she wants. Explain why he or she dreams about a different kind of career. Use any ideas you learned from the readings to help you write.

4. Share your writing with another pair. Read the other pair's report. Then answer these questions.

    a. Did the writers use complete sentences? Underline sentences you think may be incorrect. Talk it over with the writers.

    b. Is there a sentence you think is very interesting? Underline it. Tell the writers why you think it is interesting.

For step-by-step practice in the writing process, see the *Writing Activity Book, Basic/Low Intermediate, Second Edition*, Unit 1.

| | |
|---|---|
| Assignment: | Writing a Descriptive Paragraph |
| Prewriting: | Listing |
| Organizing: | Understanding Paragraphs and Topic Sentences |
| Revising: | Supporting the Topic Sentence; Using Adjectives to Give More Detail |
| Editing: | Formatting a Paragraph |

For Unit 1 Internet activities, visit the NorthStar Companion Website at http://www.longman.com/northstar.

# Country Life vs. City Life

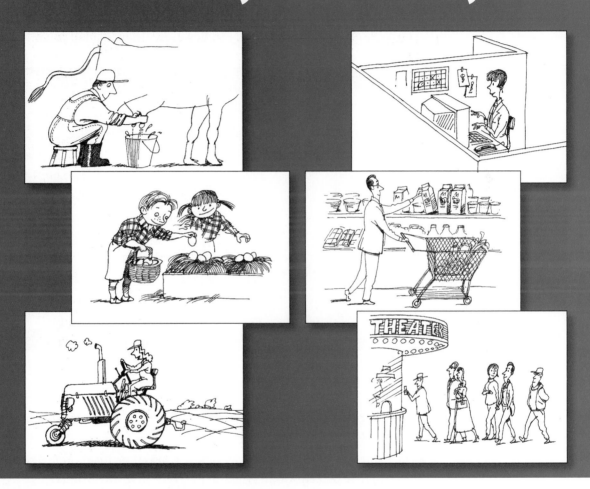

# **1** Focus on the Topic

## A PREDICTING

Look at the pictures, and discuss these questions with the class.

1. What are these people doing?

2. Where do they do these things?

3. How do you think they feel when they do these things?

# B  SHARING INFORMATION

*Work in pairs. Ask your partner the questions below. Check (✓) the right box in the chart. Share your partner's answers with the class.*

**Example:**  A: Where did your mother grow up?

B: (She grew up) in a small town.

A: *(to the class)* Mike's mother grew up in a small town.

|  | In a city | In a small town | In the country |
|---|---|---|---|
| **1.** Where did *you* grow up? |  |  |  |
| **2.** Where did your *mother* grow up? |  |  |  |
| **3.** Where did your *father* grow up? |  |  |  |
| **4.** Your *mother's mother*? |  |  |  |
| **5.** Your *mother's father*? |  |  |  |
| **6.** Your *father's mother*? |  |  |  |
| **7.** Your *father's father*? |  |  |  |

# C  PREPARING TO READ

### BACKGROUND

*Read the statements and the following questions. Write your answers to the questions, then share your answers with a partner.*

- In 1900, 50 percent of all Americans worked or lived on farms. In 2000, less than 1 percent of all Americans lived or worked on farms.

- In the late 1990s, agritourism (vacationing on small family farms) made up 5 to 10 percent of the tourist trade in Europe. Experts think this number will increase in the next 20 years.

1. Where are people living now if they are not living on farms?

_____

2. Why do you think tourists want to visit farms for their vacations? Would you like to visit a farm for your next vacation?

_____

_____

## VOCABULARY FOR COMPREHENSION

*Read each statement. Then circle the correct definition of the underlined word(s).*

1. There's a beautiful view from this window. I can watch the farmers at work in the <u>fields</u>. In winter, the fields are brown; in spring, they are green; in summer and fall, I can even see the tomatoes or pumpkins planted there.
   a. pieces of land covered with trees
   b. pieces of land for planting

2. We planted the <u>crops</u> really early this year. We got the corn, wheat, and tomatoes in the ground by the end of April.
   a. plants that a farmer grows
   b. pieces of land

3. She <u>raises</u> sheep on her farm. She is with them from the time they are born until she sells them.
   a. takes care of
   b. brings farm animals to market to sell

4. He <u>used to</u> be a farmer when he was young. After 20 years of farming, he decided to change careers. Now he's a teacher.
   a. wanted to
   b. was before but isn't now

5. Most people who live in the city find ways to enjoy <u>nature</u>. They visit the city parks, keep flowers in their windows, and go away for weekend visits to the country, to the beach, or to the mountains.
   a. activities in the city
   b. the world and everything in it which people have not made

6. Unlike most of her friends, 12-year-old Sally has a great sense of <u>responsibility</u>. She has to take care of her baby sister every day after school, and she always does it very well.
   a. something that you have to do
   b. something that you want to do

7. A lot of children from New York City have never been in a <u>wood</u>. They don't know what it's like to walk in the cool dark space where lots of plants and animals live under lots and lots of trees.
   a. park
   b. area with a large number of trees

8. They had stayed up all night. Just when they were ready to go to sleep, they saw a pink light in the sky. They decided to stay up just a little longer to watch the <u>sunrise</u>.
   a. city lights
   b. sun coming up in the morning

9. Eli's dog, Spot, is <u>dependent on</u> him. Spot needs Eli to give her food and water.
   **a.** needing someone or something to help or support you
   **b.** loving someone or something

10. Julia was at the <u>birth</u> of her first pony. She has taken care of this pony ever since the first day he came into the world.
    **a.** when a baby is born
    **b.** when someone gives something to another person

11. Mr. Gow was very <u>proud of</u> his daughter. She worked very hard for many years to start her own restaurant. Last week the newspaper said it was the best restaurant in town.
    **a.** happy that someone is making a lot of money
    **b.** happy about someone's good actions

# 2 Focus on Reading

## A    READING ONE: *The Farming Life for Me*

The reading that follows is a letter to the editor of a magazine for young people. The writer is a teenage boy who lives on a farm. He explains why he thinks it's better to grow up on a farm than to grow up in the city.

*Work with a partner. What do you think this boy's reasons are? Write a list of possible reasons.*

1. _____

2. _____

3. _____

4. _____

5. _____

*Now read the letter and see if your guesses were right.*

**Letters to the Editor   •   Letters to the Editor   •   Letters to the Editor**

## The Farming Life for Me

1    In the September 2003 issue of your magazine, you wrote that many farm kids wanted to live in the city. Well, I am a farm kid and I don't want to live in the city. In fact, I want to explain exactly why I think it's better to grow up on a farm than to grow up in the city.

2    First, farm kids are too busy with farm work to get into trouble with guns, drugs, and alcohol like a lot of city kids do. We usually go home right after school to work on the farm and help our parents. We have to milk the cows, feed all the animals, drive the tractor in the fields, fix fences, help with watering the crops, or any other kind of farm work. All these things keep us busy and out of trouble.

3    Second, farm kids understand at an early age what's really important in life. We help our parents when animals are born, and we take care of these animals until they die. I remember getting to pull my first lamb[1] when I was six. Watching the birth of an animal always makes me feel warm and happy. At the same time, I know why we raise these animals. They are going to be hamburgers and fried chicken. Like me, most farm kids are used to seeing life and death on the farm. That gives us an understanding of human life and death that city kids don't have.

4    In addition, farm kids have a much better understanding of nature than do many city kids. We work outside all year. We almost always get to watch the sunrise. We understand how heat or wind or snow can change our crops. We understand how much water different crops need at different times of year. We can put our hands in the soil[2] and know how much water it needs. We know how to choose the best trees in our woods to cut down. Those are just a few of the many outdoor skills that farm kids learn young.

5    Finally, farm kids have a greater sense of responsibility than most city kids. We know that crops and animals are totally dependent on us. We know that they can die if we don't do our work. I learned at an early age to feed and water the animals on time, and to water the crops regularly. Sometimes I'm tired or sick, or it's freezing cold or blowing snow. Even then, I know that I have to do these things because the animals, the crops, and my family depend on me.

6    For all these reasons, I think that it is better to grow up on a farm than to grow up in the city. My own experience growing up on a family farm in southern Colorado tells me this. I know that growing up on a farm made me the responsible, hardworking, and thoughtful young person my parents and community can be proud of.

*Zachary Blaine, Colorado*

[1] *pull a lamb:* to help a mother sheep when she gives birth to a baby lamb.
[2] *soil:* the dirt or earth we plant our crops in.

## READING FOR MAIN IDEAS

**1** *Check (✓) the sentence that best describes the main idea of Reading One.*

_____ **a.** Zachary believes that growing up on a farm is great for children.

_____ **b.** Zachary explains why he thinks all children should grow up on farms.

_____ **c.** Zachary explains why he thinks it's great to grow up on a farm instead of in the city.

**2** *Zachary gives four main reasons to support his idea. Choose the sentences that best express these four reasons. Label them **1–4** as they appear in the reading.*

_____ **a.** Farm children understand at an early age more about life and death than city kids.

_____ **b.** Watching the births of animals is good for farm children.

_____ **c.** Farm children understand soil better than city kids.

_____ **d.** Farm children are too busy doing farm work to get into trouble.

_____ **e.** Farm children learn to fix fences and drive tractors.

_____ **f.** Farm children understand more about nature than city children.

_____ **g.** Farm children have a greater sense of responsibility than city kids.

_____ **h.** Farm children are used to being outside more than city children.

## READING FOR DETAILS

*Read each statement. Part of the sentence is incorrect; correct it. Then write the number of the paragraph that matches this statement.*

**Paragraph**

**a.** Farm kids have to do a lot of work on the farm such as milk the cows, water the crops, and sell vegetables.                    _____

**b.** I feed and water the animals every day, and I water the crops every once in a while.                    _____

**c.** We know how to choose the worst trees in our woods to cut down.                    _____

**d.** At my house there is never enough work to do after school.                    _____

**e.** I remember the first time I saw a lamb born on our farm.                    _____

**f.** I'm not used to seeing life and death on the farm.                    _____

## REACTING TO THE READING

**1** *Read the statements, and check the ones that you think Zachary Blaine would agree with. Discuss your answers with a partner.*

_____ **1.** Farm kids would like to do the things that city kids do.

_____ **2.** Most city kids get into trouble with drugs and alcohol.

_____ **3.** Growing up with a lot of responsibility is good for kids.

_____ **4.** It's good for kids to visit places like museums, libraries, and theaters.

_____ **5.** Most city kids would like to grow up on a farm.

_____ **6.** City children might not get into trouble with guns, alcohol, and drugs if they had animals to take care of.

**2** *Read the statements in Exercise 1 again. Circle the number of the statements that you agree with. Discuss your choices with a partner. Give your opinions.*

## B    READING TWO: *Leaving the Farm*

A hundred years ago, most farmers in the United States were small farmers. Now, large farming companies do more and more of the farming. Many small farmers can't compete. They sell their farms and move their families to the city.

*Read this article about a farm family in North Dakota who recently moved to the city.*

# Leaving the Farm

**By Christopher Blum**

1   Scott Halley used to be a farmer . . . until a year ago. But the farm kept losing money. "You look at the numbers at the end of the pencil," said Mr. Halley, 44, "and you realize it's time to try something different."

2   With a heavy heart but a clear head, Mr. Halley became one of the thousands of American farmers who sell their land each year. What surprised Mr. Halley and others is that the move to the city was so easy. The farmers are finding jobs and their families are enjoying the city way of life.

3   Mr. Halley found a good job working as a scientist at North Dakota State University. His income is now double what it was when he was a farmer.

4   But even for those farmers who find good jobs, there is a price to pay in leaving farming.

5   "It's not just about making money, but about having a life that is meaningful," said Dr. Michael Rosmann, a farmer and psychologist who helps farmers. "For most of them, that grieving[1] lasts for the

[1] *grieving:* feeling very sad when we have lost somebody or something we love.

rest of their lives. To make the decision to quit farming, to do what's best for the family, takes an awful lot of courage." Mr. Halley feels the pull of the land every day. Once a week, he drives eight hours to work a small piece of his old farm, just to keep his connection to the land.

6    It was hard to leave, but Mr. Halley knows he did the right thing. For most families that leave the land, income goes up and stress from worrying about having no money goes down. Both parents and children are happier.

7    Halley's children love living in the city.

8    "The kids don't want to go back now," said Mr. Halley. "The telephone never stops ringing."

9    Megan Halley, 13, spoke with excitement about her new school. She especially likes art and computer technology. "Back on the farm," she said, "the old phone system took five minutes or more just to dial up the Internet."

10    "It's cool here," said Megan. She loves going to the nearby mall² to shop for new clothes and get the latest CDs of her favorite group. The closest store to the Halleys' farm was a ten-mile drive.

11    Before moving to the city, Megan worried about getting along with city kids.

12    "The boys here aren't any different than back in the country," she said. "There's just a lot more of them."

² **mall:** a large building with a lot of stores in it.

*Source:* Based on information in "Leaving the Farm for the Other Real World," Dirk Johnson, *The New York Times*, November 7, 1999.

*Now answer the following questions. Check your answers with a partner.*

**1.** Why does Mr. Halley drive back to his old farm once a week?

**2.** Are the Halleys happy they decided to sell the farm? Explain.

## C    LINKING READINGS ONE AND TWO

*Look at Readings One and Two again. What are the advantages and disadvantages of living in a city or living in the country? Write your answers on a separate piece of paper in a chart like the one below.*

|                    | City Living | Country Living |
| ------------------ | ----------- | -------------- |
| **1.** Advantages  |             |                |
| **2.** Disadvantages |           |                |

*Now answer the following question, and discuss it with your class.*

Where do you think it is best to raise a family, in the country or the city?

# **3** Focus on Vocabulary

**1** *The word **use** can be used in different ways and have different meanings. Read the following sentences.*

| | |
|---|---|
| **SENTENCE 1:** | I **use** a computer to write my reports. |
| **MEANING:** | *I write my reports with a computer.* |
| **DEFINITION:** | ***use:*** to do something with something (a tool, machine, etc.). |
| **SENTENCE 2:** | I **used to** live in the country. Now I live in New York City. |
| **MEANING:** | *I lived in the country in the past, but now I live in New York City.* |
| **DEFINITION:** | ***used to:*** was done in the past but is not done now. |
| **SENTENCE 3:** | I'm **used to** the noise. At first the sound of traffic kept me awake at night. After living in the city for five years, the noise doesn't bother me. |
| **MEANING:** | *At the beginning, the noise was strange to me and kept me awake at night, but now I am familiar with it and can sleep.* |
| **DEFINITION:** | ***be/get used to:*** be or become familiar with something or someone so that it does not seem strange or unusual or difficult. |

*Now complete the sentences with the correct form of **use, used to,** or **be used to.***

1. She _____ make all her own bread when she was younger.

2. Most farmers _____ waking up before the sun.

3. In the city, people _____ waiting in long lines at the bank or post office.

4. Most Americans _____ live on farms. Today most Americans live in cities or towns.

5. These days, farmers _____ machines to milk the cows.

6. Mr. Byrne doesn't like modern technology. He _____ his old coffeemaker every morning instead of the new electric one his daughter gave him for Christmas.

7. Audrey _____ hate riding the crowded bus. Now it doesn't bother her. She _____ it.

**2** *Read the clues. Complete the crossword puzzle with words from the box.*

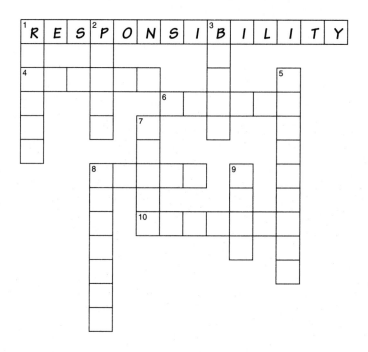

| birth | dependent | proud | responsibility |
|-------|-----------|-------|----------------|
| courage | income | quit | sunrise |
| crops | nature | raises | woods |

**Across**

1. "I don't want to take care of a dog. I don't want to worry about it or feed it or have to take it on walks." This man does not want _____ for a dog.

4. "I can't believe it. When I first started working, I made $20,000 a year. Now, I'm making around $60,000. I never thought I could do it." This man is excited because his _____ is so much higher now.

6. "Oh, I love being outside. I love to feel the wind in my face while I walk through the trees listening to the birds." He loves _____.

8. "Well, I already planted the corn. The tomatoes can't go in until April. I guess I could go out and plant the carrots and cucumbers today." This farmer is trying to decide which _____ to plant.

10. "I love this time of day. Most people are still asleep. I feel like I have the world and this beautiful view all to myself." The woman is watching the _____.

**Down**

1. "I've got more chickens than you could count. I have black ones, brown ones, gray ones. I have young ones and old ones. What kind of chicken are you looking for?" This farmer _____ chickens.

2. "I'm so happy for you. You really did such a good job. I'm just so pleased." The mother is very _____ of her son.

3. "It was just amazing. I had never seen anything so beautiful! And to hold my baby son in my arms for the first time! I'll never forget it." This man is describing the _____ of his son.

5. "I just don't know what I would do without my car. It takes me everywhere—to work, to the gym, to the store. I don't think I could live without it." This man is _____ on his car.

7. "I like to be in big open spaces. I don't really like tall buildings or even tall trees. In fact, I don't like any trees." This person would not like to walk in the _____.

8. "You are so brave. I would be too afraid to try to get a new job after being a farmer for 30 years. I just don't think I could do it." This farmer is talking to his neighbor. He thinks his neighbor has a lot of _____.

9. "I love the farm. I don't want to leave. But everyone tells me I'm losing money. They say I should sell the land and move to the city. But, I'm not ready to give it up. I'm going to stay." This farmer doesn't want to _____ farming.

**3** *You spent your vacation on your aunt's farm. Your friend visited a cousin in London. Read the letter from your friend. He asks you some questions about your vacation.*

> Dear Isaac,
>
> I had a great time on my vacation. I loved London. My cousin has a great apartment. It's small, but it's on the thirteenth floor, and it has great views. From her windows I could see all the way to Big Ben and Parliament. I kept thinking of you on your aunt's farm.
> (1) What kind of farm is it? What does she grow? Does she have animals?
>
> I saw five shows. I went to Westminster Abbey, London Bridge, and the Tower of London. Most nights, I went out to dinner and then went to a show or a movie or a concert. Or all three!

What about on the farm? **(2) What interesting things did you do or see?**

    I had a super vacation. I think I could really get used to life in a city like London! I love shopping all day and going out every night! What about you? **(3) Could you get used to life on the farm?**

    I hope you had a great time. I'll call you next week.

                                Talk to you soon,
                                Rogelio

*Now reply to your friend. Answer his questions using the words in the box.*

| be used to it | crops | quit | sunrise | used to |
| birth | fields | raise | use | woods |
| courage | proud of | responsibility | | |

Dear Rogelio,

Thanks for your letter. It sounds like London was fantastic. It sounds so different from my vacation. I must say though, I had a great time on Aunt Lisa's farm.

(1) It's a small farm, but . . . _____

_____

_____

(2) I did some very exciting things. For instance, one day . . . _____

_____

_____

(3) Yes, I certainly could get used to life on a farm. I love . . . _____

_____

_____

Well, that's all I can think of for now. I can't wait to see you!

See you soon,

Isaac

# 4 Focus on Writing

## A  STYLE:  The Paragraph

**1** *Look at the following passage. Don't read the text. Just look at it. How many paragraphs do you see? How do you know a paragraph has stopped or started?*

The Farm School in Athol, Massachusetts, is a working farm that takes in schoolchildren. They stay for three days to learn about life on a farm, to taste a little bit of nature, and to understand the value of hard work. With help from the Farm School teachers, the children do the work of farmers: They milk the cows; plant the vegetables; collect the eggs; make cheese; brush Mac, the horse; or fix buildings and fences.

The kids love the work. They love the feeling of being able to see the work they did with their own hands. They are excited to make things with their hands using ideas they studied back at school. A group of students who built a fence out of wood from the farm's trees said proudly, "We really used math." Working on the farm makes kids feel great about themselves and their hard work.

### The Paragraph

A **paragraph** is two or more sentences about one main idea.

1. The main idea usually appears in the first sentence, called the **topic sentence.**

TOPIC S.
The kids love the work.

2. The following sentences in the paragraph explain or discuss the main idea. They might give examples of the main idea or explain why the main idea is true. These are called **supporting sentences.**

SUPPORTING S.1
They love the feeling of being able to see the work they did with their own hands.

SUPPORTING S.2
They are excited to make things with their hands using ideas they studied back in school.

3. Sometimes at the end of the paragraph, there is a sentence that repeats the main idea of the paragraph. This is called the **concluding sentence.**

CONCLUDING S.
Working on the farm makes kids feel great about themselves and their hard work.

When writing a paragraph, indent the first sentence five spaces.

The Farm School in Athol, Massachusetts, is a working farm that takes in school children . . .

**2** *Each one of these paragraphs is missing a topic sentence. Read each incomplete paragraph. Then choose the best topic sentence from the list below. Write it on the line.*

1. _____

One way is to spend time in the parks. Most cities have large open parks where you can run, play soccer, or just enjoy nature. Another way is to grow plants in pots. You can even grow vegetables in pots. Living in the city doesn't mean you can't enjoy nature.

**a.** People can enjoy nature in a few different ways.
**b.** There are a few ways for country people to enjoy nature.
**c.** There are a couple of ways to stay in touch with nature while living in the city.

2. _____

He writes about his land, farming, and American life. He has written over 30 books. Berry lives on a small farm in Kentucky with his wife, Tanya. He uses his own hands or animals to do most of the work on the farm. He grows most of his own food, and he buys what he can't grow from his neighbors. His writing is often about his land, his farm, or his town.

**a.** Wendell Berry is a writer.
**b.** Wendell Berry lives on a farm in Kentucky.
**c.** Wendell Berry is an American writer and farmer.

**3** *Read each topic sentence below. From the list of possible supporting sentences, choose three that you think work* best *with each topic sentence. Show the order by writing* **1, 2,** *or* **3** *next to the sentences.*

1. The children who visit the Farm School love being in nature.

_____ **a.** They learn to see things they never noticed in the land around them.

_____ **b.** "I loved learning how to build a fence," said one girl.

_____ **c.** "I never saw light come through the leaves," said one young girl.

_____ **d.** They love not having homework for three days.

_____ **e.** "I watched my first sunrise. I never knew it was so beautiful," said another.

2. American farm families are starting to act more like city families.

_____ **a.** British farmers are selling their farms in record numbers.

_____ **b.** Farm children start working in the fields at a young age.

_____ **c.** Dad usually stays working the farm and Mom gets a job in town.

_____ **d.** With more wives working off the farm, a lot of farm families now eat out in restaurants just like city families.

_____ **e.** Most farm families now have both parents working.

**4** *The following should be written as two paragraphs. Read it carefully, and put a check (✓) before the sentence that you think starts the second paragraph.*

In general, tourists love the Appleby's Farm Stay. _____ Most of the visitors talk about the wonderful food Mrs. Appleby serves for dinner and breakfast. _____ They think it's so fresh and so delicious. _____ Everyone talks about the beautiful walks through the fields and woods. _____ The children who visit love watching Mr. Appleby milk the cows and lead them in and out of the barn. _____ On the other hand, the Appleby's Farm Stay is not the vacation for everyone. _____ The rooms at the Appleby's are very plain with a bathroom down the hall. _____ You can't choose what food you want to eat. _____ You eat what the family eats.

_____ Also, not everyone likes to walk around all the animals you find on the Appleby's farm. _____ Some tourists are just city people. _____ Farm Stays, even the lovely Appleby's Farm Stay, are definitely not for them.

**5** *Use the topic sentence provided below to write a paragraph with four supporting sentences.*

I love visiting a large city because there are so many interesting things to do.

_____

_____

_____

_____

_____

_____

## B    GRAMMAR: Simple Past Tense

**1** *Read the following paragraph. Underline the verbs that tell about the past. Then answer the questions.*

Ben Holmes started the Farm School in 1991. Holmes, a city kid from California, spent summers on his uncle's farm in Ohio. There he learned to love working on the land. He created the school because he wanted to teach kids that work is about using your body and your mind together.

**1.** How is the simple past formed for most verbs (regular verbs)?

**2.** Which past tense verb is irregular? What is the base form of this verb?

## Simple Past Tense

1. When we talk about things that happened in the past, we use the **simple past tense.**

   Last summer, I **worked** on a farm.
   I **went** to the city yesterday.

| Base Form | Simple Past |
|---|---|
| | |

2. To form the simple past tense for **regular** verbs, add **-ed** to the base form of the verb.

| Base Form | Simple Past |
|---|---|
| want | want**ed** |
| talk | talk**ed** |

   If the verb ends in **e,** add only **-d.**

| | |
|---|---|
| live | live**d** |
| arrive | arrive**d** |

   If the verb ends in consonant + **y,** change the **y** to **i** and then add **-ed.**

| | |
|---|---|
| study | stud**ied** |
| try | tr**ied** |

3. Many verbs have **irregular** past tense forms. Here are some of these irregular verbs.

| | |
|---|---|
| be | **was / were** |
| do | **did** |
| have | **had** |
| eat | **ate** |
| get | **got** |
| go | **went** |
| make | **made** |
| say | **said** |

4. In negative statements, use **didn't (did not)** + base form of the verb, except with the verb *be.*

| | |
|---|---|
| need | **didn't** need |
| want | **didn't** want |
| be | **wasn't / weren't** |

**2** *Read Toby's letter. Complete it with the simple past tense forms of the verbs. Some of the verbs are regular and some are irregular.*

Dear Ayla,

I just _____ back from the fifth-grade class trip to the
        1. get
farm. It _____ great. I'm so tired. You wouldn't believe
        2. be
what we did in just three days. On the first day, the teachers

_____ us all over the farm and we each _____
3. show                                              4. get

a chance to milk the cow, Daisy.  After we _____ lunch,
5. eat

I _____ with some other students to the barn. There we
6. go

_____ the horses. After dinner, the teachers _____
7. brush                                                   8. play

music and we _____ for hours.
9. dance

We _____ really early the second day and _____
10. wake up                                     11. plant

tomatoes all morning. After lunch, we _____ stones from
12. carry

the field. That _____ hard! After dinner the second night,
13. be

everyone _____ too tired to dance. We just _____
14. be                                              15. talk

around the fire before bed.

I miss you and hope to hear from you soon.

Toby

**3** *Write answers to the following questions using the simple past tense.*

1. When did you last go the country?

2. What did you do there?

3. What did you want to do that you didn't do?

## C  WRITING TOPICS

*Choose one of the following topics. Write one or two paragraphs. Use the vocabulary, grammar, and style that you learned in this unit.*

1. Look at the exercise Linking Readings One and Two on page 26. Use the information in the chart to write two paragraphs. One paragraph should describe the advantages and disadvantages of city living. The other should describe the advantages and disadvantages of country living.

2. Which do you think is better, country life or city life? Write a short paragraph to give your opinion.

3. Have you ever spent time on a farm? Using the simple past tense, write a paragraph to describe your visit. Consider these questions: What did you expect to see or do? Did you see or do those things? What do you remember the most? What was difficult or uncomfortable? What was the most interesting or least interesting part of your visit?

## D RESEARCH TOPIC

*What is it like to live on a farm? Find out. Follow these steps.*

1. Interview someone who at one point in his or her life lived on a farm. Ask this person to tell you about the day-to-day activities on the farm. You could start with the following questions and then ask questions of your own. Take notes.

   a. When did you live on this farm?

   b. Where was the farm?

   c. What time did you usually wake up?

   d. What did you do before breakfast?

   e. When did you eat breakfast?

   f. What was the hardest thing you did on the farm?

   g. What did you like best?

   h. _____

   i. _____

2. Write a paragraph using the simple past tense to describe one usual day in the life of the people living on that farm. Use the information you collected.

3. Share your writing with a partner. Read your partner's paragraph. Then answer these questions.

   a. Did the writer indent the first line in the paragraph?

   b. Did the writer start the paragraph with a topic sentence?

   c. Did the writer use the simple past tense correctly? Underline any verbs you think may be incorrect. Talk it over with your partner.

   d. Is there a sentence you think is very interesting? Underline it. Tell your partner why you think it's interesting.

---

For step-by-step practice in the writing process, see the *Writing Activity Book, Basic/Low Intermediate, Second Edition,* Unit 2.

| | |
|---|---|
| Assignment: | Writing a Descriptive Paragraph |
| Prewriting: | Using Pictures |
| Organizing: | Grouping Details |
| Revising: | Adding Supporting Details; Writing About Past Events |
| Editing: | Using Commas and Periods |

For Unit 2 Internet activities, visit the NorthStar Companion Website at http://www.longman.com/northstar.

# Making Money

U.S. $100 bill before 1996

U.S. $100 bill after 1996

# 1 Focus on the Topic

## A PREDICTING

Look at the bills, and discuss these questions with the class.

1. Why do you think the $100 bill was changed?

2. What differences can you see between the two bills?

# B    SHARING INFORMATION

*What do you think about the following actions? Are they acceptable? Are they wrong? Some things may seem more wrong to you than others. For each action, check (✓) the box that shows what you think. Compare your answers in a small group.*

| Actions | Acceptable | Not so wrong | Wrong | Very wrong |
|---|---|---|---|---|
| **1.** A student doesn't want to buy a book he needs, so he copies some chapters on a copy machine. | | | | |
| **2.** A student copies a friend's paper and gives it to her teacher with her own name on it. | | | | |
| **3.** A man finds a bag with $50 in it. He keeps the money. | | | | |
| **4.** A man needs some money. He copies paper money on a copy machine. | | | | |
| **5.** A girl needs some money. She takes $5 from her mother's wallet. | | | | |
| **6.** A man borrows $10 from a friend and never repays him. | | | | |

# C    PREPARING TO READ

## BACKGROUND

When you read a story, there may be many words you don't know. Often you can still understand the story, and sometimes you can even understand these new words.

*Read the following story. See if you can understand it even though some words are missing.*

One day in 1993, some New York City garbage workers were very surprised when they emptied a trash can. Along with the banana peels and empty Coke cans, they found $18 million in new (**1**) _____.

Who would throw out all that money? The workers felt that something was not right, so they called the United States Bureau of Engraving and Printing, the part of government that makes paper money. The Bureau employees said that the money looked real but that it was actually (2) _____—and not legal. The garbage belonged to (3) _____, people who make money that is not real. They make the money by using printing presses, big machines similar to those for making books or newspapers, or by using (4) _____ and other computer (5) _____. These counterfeiters probably printed a lot of money and weren't happy with how it looked. Maybe the drawing wasn't good enough. So they threw it all out. The Bureau of Engraving and Printing employees were mad because they didn't know if the counterfeiters were able to (6) _____ the drawings and go on to make another $18 million that looked (7) _____ real.

*Now answer these questions. Then discuss your answers with a classmate.*

1. What did the New York City garbage workers find?

   _____

2. Who threw out all that money?

   _____

## VOCABULARY FOR COMPREHENSION

*Read the story again. Work with a partner. Use information in the story to guess the meaning of the missing words. Write your guesses on the lines that follow.*

1. _____
2. _____
3. _____
4. _____
5. _____
6. _____
7. _____

*Now read the story with the vocabulary words filled in.*

One day in 1993, some New York City garbage workers were very surprised when they emptied a trash can. Along with the banana peels and empty Coke cans, they found $18 million in new (**1**) <u>bills</u>.

Who would throw out all that money? The workers felt that something was not right, so they called the United States Bureau of Engraving and Printing, the part of government that makes paper money. The Bureau employees said that the money looked real but that it was actually (**2**) <u>fake</u>—and not legal. The garbage belonged to (**3**) <u>counterfeiters</u>, people who make money that is not real. They make the money by using printing presses similar to those for making books or newspapers, or by using (**4**) <u>scanners</u> and other computer (**5**) <u>equipment</u>. These counterfeiters probably printed a lot of money and weren't happy with how it looked. Maybe the drawing wasn't good enough. So they threw it all out. The Bureau of Engraving and Printing employees were mad because they didn't know if the counterfeiters were able to (**6**) <u>improve</u> the drawings and go on to make another $18 million that looked (**7**) <u>completely</u> real.

*Work with the class. Make a list of the new vocabulary words. Together write one definition that seems best for each word.*

# 2 Focus on Reading

## A   READING ONE: *Making Money*

The following article is about how counterfeiters make fake money. It is also about how the U.S. government tries to stop counterfeiting.

*Work in a small group. Make a list of things that you think the government might do to make money harder to copy.*

1. _____
2. _____
3. _____
4. _____
5. _____
6. _____
7. _____
8. _____

*Now read the article. Were your ideas correct?*

# MAKING MONEY

**By Amelia Laidlaw**

1 It was so quick and easy. A 14-year-old boy in Scottsdale, Arizona, pulled out a $50 bill and put it onto his school's new computer scanner. Then he printed ten copies of his  $50 bill on a color copier. Within seconds he changed $50 into $550, and he was ready to shop.

2 Twenty years ago only a few people had the skills or equipment to make counterfeit money. Computer, copier, and printer technology has improved so much that today almost anyone can "make" money. With the new technology there is a new kind of counterfeiter: casual counterfeiters. These counterfeiters are called casual because they don't have special skills and because they don't need to plan much.

3 The number of fake bills made by casual counterfeiters on their home or office computer is growing fast. In fact, this number has doubled every year since 1989! There is no way to completely prevent counterfeiting. However, the government has recently found a few ways to make casual counterfeiting more difficult than ever before.

4 One way is to put very, very small words, called microprint, in hidden places on the bill. These words are only 6/1,000 inch. No one can read them without a magnifying glass, a special glass that makes things look bigger. And they are too small to come out clearly on a copier. If someone copies a bill that has microprint and you look at the copy through a magnifying glass, instead of microprinted words, you will see only black lines.

5 Another way to prevent people from making counterfeit money on their home computers is to use special color-changing ink. Money printed with color-changing ink will look green from one angle and yellow from another. Home computers cannot use color-changing ink. So any copies from a home computer will have normal ink and can be noticed quite easily.

6 Additionally, money is made on special paper with very small pieces of red and blue silk mixed in. And on each bill there is a special line that runs from the top to the bottom of the bill. Suppose, for example, that you hold a $20 bill up to the light. If you do this, you can see the line has the words "USA twenty." The line turns red if you put it under a special (ultraviolet) light. This line and the special paper with red and blue silk are not easy for home computers to copy.

7 The government must try many different ways to stop counterfeiting. The Bureau of Engraving and Printing needs to keep changing the way money is made because counterfeiters can learn to copy the changes. Today copiers can't copy microprinted words or color-changing ink. But, in a few years, who knows?

## READING FOR MAIN IDEAS

**1** *The following sentences tell the main ideas of the seven paragraphs in "Making Money."*
*Read the sentences. For each, write the correct paragraph number.*

**Paragraph**

**a.** Casual counterfeiting is becoming a big problem, and
the government is fighting the problem.                          _____

**b.** Color-changing ink is a way to prevent counterfeiting.     _____

**c.** A child can easily copy paper money.                       _____

**d.** The government must always keep changing the bills
to prevent people from counterfeiting.                          _____

**e.** Microprint is a way to prevent counterfeiting.             _____

**f.** New technology makes casual counterfeiting possible.       _____

**g.** Special paper and a special line are two ways to prevent
counterfeiting.                                                 _____

**2** *Check (✓) the sentence that best describes the main idea of the whole article.*

_____   **a.** It's easier to counterfeit money today than it was 20 years ago.

_____   **b.** The government has several ways to try to prevent counterfeiting.

_____   **c.** New technology makes counterfeiting easier, but the government has
changed bills to make counterfeiting more difficult.

## READING FOR DETAILS

*Complete the sentences with information from the article.*

**1.** Twenty years ago, only a few people had the _____ or
_____ to make fake money.

**2.** One way to prevent counterfeiters from making fake money on a
_____ is to use microprinted words.

**3.** Bills have a _____ that you can see if you hold them up to
the light.

**4.** Bills are printed on special paper that has pieces of _____ and
_____ silk.

5. A boy in Scottsdale, Arizona, used his school's scanner to make

_____ copies of a $ _____ bill.

6. Money printed with color-changing ink looks green from one angle and

_____ from another.

## REACTING TO THE READING

**1** *Which of the following statements do you think are true? Write **T** (true) or **F** (false). Discuss your answers with a partner.*

_____ **1.** Most casual counterfeiters make a lot of money.

_____ **2.** The government is concerned about casual counterfeiters.

_____ **3.** Most casual counterfeiters are caught by the police.

_____ **4.** Today, most counterfeit money is made by casual counterfeiters.

_____ **5.** The government changes the way it makes money every few years.

_____ **6.** Copiers will be able to copy microprint in just a few years.

**2** *Discuss the following questions in a small group. Give your opinions.*

1. Before you read this article, did you know about counterfeiting and what the government does to stop it?

2. Do people where you live check for counterfeit bills?

3. Why are dollars copied more often than other currencies?

4. Can you think of other things governments can do to prevent counterfeiting?

5. What would you do if you saw someone copying money on a public copier?

6. What would you do if you found a fake bill in your wallet?

## B    READING TWO: *I Made It Myself*

Before computers and copiers, counterfeiting was not easy. You needed the artistic skill to draw a copy of a bill, a large printing press, and the skill to use it. Counterfeiting often took a lot of time, planning, and hard work. Still the results were excellent. The counterfeit money looked and felt like the real thing. Today, professional counterfeiters still make fake money the old-fashioned way—on printing presses.

*Now turn to page 44 and read the story of Michael Landress, who was once a professional counterfeiter.*

# I MADE IT MYSELF

1    It took months of planning, of trying to find the perfect paper, of mixing and remixing ink to get the right color, of printing and reprinting to get the right feel, but I did it. I made a perfect copy of a $100 bill.

2    During the days, I did regular print jobs at the shop. Then every evening at five o'clock, I sent my workers home, hoping no one would ask why I stayed late. I pulled out the paper, ink, and other equipment I hid away the night before and slowly, carefully worked until the sun came up. I didn't have time to sleep. I was too nervous to sleep anyway. As I worked, I worried about the Secret Service[1] agents coming to get me. In the beginning, as I prepared the paper, I said to myself, "I'm just printing little blue and red hair lines on paper. They can't arrest me for that." Then as I printed the numbers, I said, "I'm just printing small numbers in four corners of a page. They can't arrest me for *this*." Finally, as I got closer and closer to printing something I could be arrested for, I began to

wonder, "Is this really that bad? Who am I hurting? I'm making myself a few thousand dollars so I can take my boy and move to Puerto Rico. I'm just trying to do my best for my family. Is that so wrong?"

3    After about three weeks of slow work, I finally printed out a whole sheet of $100 bills. I took out the magnifying glass and studied my work. "No. Oh, Ben, no. Ben, you don't look right," I said aloud to the empty shop. The portrait[2] of Ben Franklin on the front of the bill just didn't look right. To most people, he probably looked like the one on the real bill. However, I could see that it wasn't a perfect copy. I needed it to be perfect. So, slowly, painfully, I started over.

4    A week later, I was printing the last of the bills. I didn't hear them come in because of the noise of the press. I just looked up from studying the now-perfect portraits of Ben Franklin to see a gun at my head and hear the Secret Service agent say, "Just like getting caught with your hand in the cookie jar, huh, Mike?"

---

[1] *Secret Service:* government agency that tries to find and catch counterfeiters.
[2] *portrait:* a drawing or painting of someone's head.

*Source:* Based on M. M. Landress with Bruce Dobler, *I Made It Myself* (New York: Grosset and Dunlap, 1973).

*Now answer the following questions. Check your answers with a partner.*

1. The title of the story is *I Made It Myself*. What does "It" refer to?

2. In the third paragraph, Landress says, "No. Oh, Ben, no." Who is Ben? What was wrong?

3. In the fourth paragraph, Landress says, "I didn't hear them come in because of the noise of the press." Who does "them" refer to?

4. The story ends with "Just like getting caught with your hand in the cookie jar, huh, Mike?" What do you think "getting caught with your hand in the cookie jar" means?

## C    LINKING READINGS ONE AND TWO

There are two kinds of counterfeiters: casual counterfeiters, like the 14-year-old boy in Scottsdale, Arizona, and professional counterfeiters like Mike Landress.

*Based on Readings One and Two, compare the two kinds of counterfeiters. For each statement, check (✓) the right box in the chart. Explain your answers to your classmates.*

| | Casual counterfeiters | Professional counterfeiters |
|---|---|---|
| 1. Make fake money more quickly | | |
| 2. Make better-looking fake money | | |
| 3. Won't be affected by microprint | | |
| 4. Make fake money that really feels like real money | | |
| 5. Need special skills | | |
| 6. Do much more counterfeiting than they did 20 years ago | | |
| 7. Can get caught more easily | | |

# 3 Focus on Vocabulary

**1** *The sentences below do not make sense. Replace the underlined word or phrase with the antonym (or opposite of that word) from the box so the sentences make sense.*

| | | | |
|---|---|---|---|
| arrested | completely | fake | nervous |
| casual | counterfeit | improved | prevent |

1. When I bought the jeans, he told me they were Levi's. But when I got home, I saw that the Levi's name was not on the pocket. These were <u>real</u> Levi's *counterfeit* jeans.

2. Look at this bill. The ink is almost brown, not green. The paper feels like regular computer paper, not money. This must be the work of a <u>professional</u> counterfeiter.

3. The police officer took the woman by the arms, put her in the police car, and took her to the police station. He <u>set</u> her <u>free</u>.

4. Look at her diamond necklace. I can see scratch marks. It doesn't shine in the light. I think it's <u>real</u>.

5. His legs were shaking. His heart was going very fast. His lips were dry. He felt very <u>relaxed</u> as he gave the bank the counterfeit money.

6. The fire destroyed everything in the house. Everything that mattered to the family—the photos, the important papers, the furniture—was <u>not at all</u> destroyed.

7. Her English has <u>gotten worse</u>. She speaks more quickly and more smoothly. Her pronunciation is much better. And she seems more comfortable talking in English.

8. After you catch a cold, there is little to do but wait for it to go away. But there are several things you can do to <u>cause</u> colds. You can wash your hands a lot, not share cups or dishes with sick people, get enough sleep, and drink a lot of water.

**2** *Complete the sentences with the words from the box.*

| arrest | casual | fake | nervous | scanner |
|--------|--------|------|---------|---------|
| bill | equipment | improve | prevent | skill |

1. Printing presses, copiers, scanners, ink, and magnifying glasses are different kinds of _____ used in counterfeiting.

2. Driving carefully can _____ a lot of car accidents.

3. Everyone liked the artist's work and thought it showed great _____.

4. I want to be able to put this photograph on my computer screen. I need a(n) _____.

5. Don't be fooled by that "Rolex" watch. It's cheap because it's a(n) _____.

6. I need change. Can I have four quarters for a one-dollar _____?

7. He's very _____ about his business—I don't think he takes it at all seriously.

8. My teacher said the best way to _____ my English is to visit an English-speaking country.

9. All counterfeiters must feel very _____ the first time they try to spend their fake money in a store.

10. We can't _____ every casual counterfeiter we catch. Many of them are children just having fun.

**3** *Read the following information.*

Imagine you are a reporter who is writing an article on counterfeiting. You are interviewing bankers. You want to find out how banks deal with counterfeit money and counterfeiters.

*Use the following words to write four questions you might ask a bank manager. Use at least one of these words in each question.*

| | | | |
|---|---|---|---|
| arrest | counterfeiter(s) | improve | professional |
| bill | equipment | nervous | scanner |
| completely | fake | prevent | technology |
| counterfeit | | | |

**Example:**   How often do you catch a <u>counterfeiter</u>?

1. _____

2. _____

3. _____

4. _____

# 4 Focus on Writing

## A    STYLE: Transition Words of Addition and Contrast

**1** *Read the paragraph and answer the questions that follow.*

    Small-time thieves have a couple of ways to make counterfeit money quickly. For example, they cut off the numbers from the four corners of a $20 bill and glue them onto the corner of four $1 bills. <u>Also, they copy a $50 bill on a color copier and try to use the copy as real money. However, these people are easy to catch. Only professional counterfeiters can make bills that look real.</u>

    **1.** Which underlined sentence adds information that is similar to information in the sentence before it?

    _____

    **2.** Which underlined sentence adds information that is different from information in the sentence before it?

    _____

## Transition Words

Transition words of addition and contrast help you connect sentences when you compare two things.

1. **Transition words of addition** connect two sentences that have similar ideas. These transitions include *in addition, additionally, also,* and *too.*

Money is made on special paper. **Also,** on each bill there is a special line that runs from the top to the bottom.

2. **Transition words of contrast** connect two sentences that have opposite ideas. These transitions include *however, in contrast,* and *on the other hand.*

There is no way to completely prevent counterfeiting. **However,** the government has recently found a few ways to make it more difficult.

3. Transition words usually come at the **beginning** of the sentence. But the transition word *too* always comes at the **end** of the sentence. Transition words are usually separated from the rest of the sentence by a **comma.**

U.S. dollar bills have microprinted words. **In addition,** they have color-changing ink. They have special paper, **too.**

**2** *Complete the paragraphs with appropriate transition words. More than one answer is possible. Share your paragraphs with a partner.*

There have been many changes made to the U.S. $100 bill. The portrait has changed. The ink has changed, (1) _____. (2) _____, the size and color of the bills have not changed.

The new $100 bill has a larger portrait of Ben Franklin. This picture is easier to see, and the added detail is harder to copy. (3) _____, the portrait is now off center to make room for a watermark[1] and to prevent the portrait from getting wrinkled.

The ink has been changed from a single-color ink to a color-shifting ink. This ink will appear green from one angle and yellow from another.

These changes help make the bills more difficult to copy. (4) _____, some things have not changed. For example, the

---

[1] *watermark:* a design put into paper that can only be seen when held up to the light.

bill is still 6 inches by 2½ inches. The paper is still a cotton/linen mix.
(5) _____, the colors remain black on the front of the bill and
green on the back. (6) _____, because of the color-shifting ink,
the green does change a little when you look at it from a different angle.

**3** *In the correct order, the following sentences make up a paragraph. Use your understanding of transitions to put these sentences into the correct order. Show the order by writing **1, 2,** or **3** next to each.*

_____ **a.** Also, you can run your hand over the bill. Sometimes people glue higher numbers onto $1 bills. You can easily feel these bills right away.

_____ **b.** Sometimes it's easy to tell if your money is counterfeit. You can look at the microprinted words under a magnifying glass. If you can read them, your money should be real.

_____ **c.** On the other hand, it's sometimes very difficult to tell if money is counterfeit. If a professional made the counterfeit bills, you won't feel anything unusual and you might be able to read the microprinted words.

**4** *Read the following information.*

Your boss has asked you to buy an anticounterfeiting tool. You looked at a few and decided that the electronic cash scanner was the best one. You read the advertisements about it and took the notes below.

*Now your boss wants a short report on why you chose this tool. Use the transition words of addition and contrast to write your report (one paragraph).*

| THE ELECTRONIC CASH SCANNER |
| --- |
| It's easy to use. You just put the bills in the machine and wait for the machine to electronically scan them. |
| It's very easy to tell if money is counterfeit. A red light flashes and an alarm sounds. |
| It will last a long time. It should work for at least ten years. |
| It's expensive. It costs $525. |

## B    GRAMMAR: Comparative Form of Adjectives

**1** *Read the following advertisement. Underline all the words that end in* **-er.** *Then answer the questions that follow.*

### COUNTERFEIT MONEY DETECTOR

**Protect your business against counterfeit money!**

Our new machine for checking bills is faster than the old machines. And our machine is easier than the old machines. All you do is put a bill in the machine. If the bill is counterfeit, an alarm bell will ring. It's as easy as that! Counterfeit protection is here. Buy the ***Counterfeit Money Detector*** today, and you can sleep well tonight.

You have to be smarter than the counterfeiters! Buy our machine.

**Counterfeit Money Detector—$450**
**Call today. Call 1-800-12-MONEY**

1. What three words did you underline?

   _____

   _____

   _____

2. What word follows each of these words?

   _____

## Comparative Form of Adjectives

The words you underlined are adjectives in the **comparative form.**

**1.** Use the comparative form of adjectives to compare two people, places, or things.

Our new machine is **faster** than the old machine.
You have to be **smarter** than the counterfeiters.

**2.** If the adjective has one syllable, add **-er** to make the comparative. Add only **-r** if the word ends in **e.**

fast        fast**er**
old         old**er**
large       large**r**

**3.** When a one-syllable adjective ends in a consonant + vowel + consonant, double the last consonant and add **-er.**

big         big**ger**
hot         hot**ter**

**4.** If a two-syllable adjective ends in **-y,** change **y** to **i** and add **-er.**

easy        eas**ier**
busy        bus**ier**

**5.** Some adjectives have irregular comparative forms.

good        **better**
bad         **worse**

**6.** For most adjectives that have two or more syllables, add **more** before the adjective to make the comparative.

In the past it was **more difficult** than it is today to counterfeit money.

**7.** Use **than** after the comparative form and before the second person, place, or thing. If the second person, place, or thing is understood, do not use **than.**

Dixon is **faster than** Amy.
This machine is **more expensive than** that one.
Bart doesn't like his bicycle. He wants to buy one that is **faster.**

**2** *Two high school students are bored in class, so they are passing notes back and forth on a piece of paper. Read the notes on page 53. Complete the notes with the comparative form of the adjective provided.*

Can you believe how boring this class is? Aargh! This is even ___*more boring*___
                                                            1. (boring)

than Shoemaker's history class!

*Yeah. I'm almost asleep over here. Did you hear what Tom did last weekend? Wow.*

*It's _____ than anything I've ever done.*
                2. (bad)

No. What?

*You know that old car of his? He really wanted to buy a _____*
                                                       3. (good)

*one. But he didn't have any money. So guess what he did?*

He stole money from his parents?

*No, he did something much _____ than that! He copied a $100*
                                              4. (crazy)

*bill on his family's new scanner and printed it out with their color printer.*

Wow! Doesn't he know counterfeiting is illegal?

*I know. I told him. But he said he's _____ than most car*
                                                5. (smart)

*salesmen. He says they won't even know the money is fake.*

This is _____ than anything he's ever done. He could go to jail!
               6. (dangerous)

*I know. I told him all that, too. He just said making money this way is*

*_____ and _____ than getting a job.*
              7. (easy)                                        8. (fast)

*Can you believe it?*

Tom's crazy! He's really going too far this time!

**3** *Read the following descriptions of two anticounterfeit machines. Then write sentences comparing these two machines. Use the adjectives in the list below to help you.*

| Electronic Cash Scanner | Currency Validator Pen |
|---|---|
| $525 | $19.95 |
| Will last for 10 years | Will test up to 5,000 bills |
| To use: Place bills in machine and wait a few seconds for machine to electronically scan them. | To use: Make a small dot on each bill with the pen. Wait for the color to turn dark brown (counterfeit) or to turn yellow (good). |
| If bills are counterfeit, a red light flashes and an alarm sounds. | If bills are counterfeit, a dark spot appears on bill. |

| | | | |
|---|---|---|---|
| bad | easy (to use) | good | small |
| cheap | expensive | large | strong |
| difficult (to use) | fast | slow | |

1. *The electronic cash scanner is stronger than the currency validator pen.*

2. _____

3. _____

4. _____

5. _____

6. _____

7. _____

8. _____

9. _____

10. _____

11. _____

## C  WRITING TOPICS

*Choose one of the following topics. Write one paragraph. Use some of the vocabulary, grammar, and style that you learned in this unit.*

1. Compare casual counterfeiters to professional counterfeiters. Use the information from the readings and from the exercises.

2. Suppose that you work in a store and that your boss has asked you to choose an anticounterfeiting tool for the store and to write him a note about it. You have decided the store should buy the cash scanner.

   Look back at the preceding exercise. Find one sentence you wrote that gives a reason why the pen is better. Find three sentences that give reasons why the scanner is better. Use these sentences and three transition words to write the note.

3. The word *counterfeit* applies to anything fake. For example, you can buy counterfeit Levi's jeans, counterfeit music CDs, or counterfeit computer software.

   Making counterfeit computer software is a crime. People copy expensive software and then sell it for less than it costs in the stores. Compare counterfeiting computer software to counterfeiting money. Which one is more difficult? Which is a more serious crime? Explain.

## D  RESEARCH TOPIC

*Find out how banks look for counterfeit money and what they do when they find it. To get this information, your class will write letters to several banks. Follow these steps.*

1. In a small group, prepare a list of questions for your letters. Choose the best questions from each student's answers to Exercise 3, page 48. Add more questions if needed.

2. In pairs, write your letters in correct business letter format (see Unit 4, Section 2A, page 61). In the letter, follow these steps:

   a. Address the letter to the Bank Branch Manager.

   b. Introduce yourselves. Explain that you are writing this letter for a class assignment, and that you want to learn what banks do about counterfeit money.

   c. Ask your questions.

   d. Give your teacher's name and the school's mailing address so someone at the bank can send you an answer.

   e. Thank the branch manager for taking the time to read your letter and answer you.

3. Choose several different banks to send the letters to. The banks can be local—or can even be in other countries.

4. Before you send your letter, share it with another pair. Read the other pair's letter and make sure it is correct.

For step-by-step practice in the writing process, see the *Writing Activity Book, Basic/Low Intermediate, Second Edition,* Unit 3.

| | |
|---|---|
| Assignment: | Writing a Comparison and Contrast Paragraph |
| Prewriting: | Making a Chart |
| Organizing: | Comparing and Contrasting |
| Revising: | Giving Explanations |
| | Making Comparisons with Adjectives |
| Editing: | Punctuating Transition Words of Addition and Contrast |

For Unit 3 Internet activities, visit the NorthStar Companion Website at http://www.longman.com/northstar.

# Save the Elephants

Dinosaur
Pterodactyl
Mammoth
Elephant
Owl
Horse
Crow
Deer
Panda
Tiger

## **1** Focus on the Topic

**A** PREDICTING

Look at the picture, and discuss these questions with the class.

1. Which animals do you know?

2. Which of these animals have you seen only in pictures?

3. Which of these animals have you actually seen? Where did you see them?

## B    SHARING INFORMATION

Some of the animals on page 57 are extinct (not alive anymore). Some are endangered (only a small number are still alive). And some are not in any danger.

*Work in a small group. Share what you know about the animals. Try to put each animal in the correct list.*

| Extinct | Endangered | Not in Danger |
|---------|------------|---------------|
|         |            |               |

## C    PREPARING TO READ

### BACKGROUND

*Read these Web pages. Then work in a small group and discuss the questions that follow.*

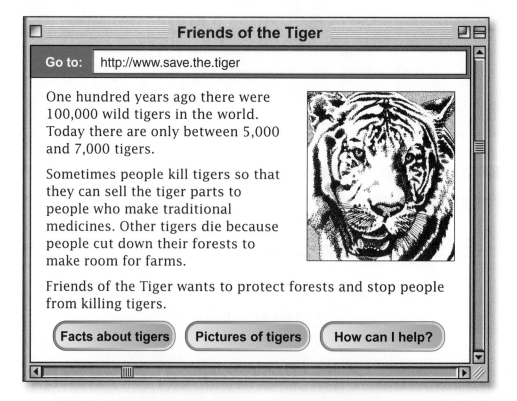

**Friends of the Tiger**

Go to:   http://www.save.the.tiger

One hundred years ago there were 100,000 wild tigers in the world. Today there are only between 5,000 and 7,000 tigers.

Sometimes people kill tigers so that they can sell the tiger parts to people who make traditional medicines. Other tigers die because people cut down their forests to make room for farms.

Friends of the Tiger wants to protect forests and stop people from killing tigers.

( Facts about tigers )    ( Pictures of tigers )    ( How can I help? )

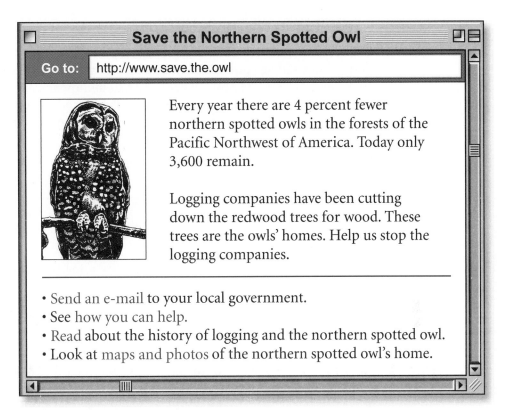

1. Why are these animals endangered?

2. What are Friends of the Tiger and Save the Northern Spotted Owl trying to do?

3. Do you think it is important to save endangered animals? Why or why not?

## VOCABULARY FOR COMPREHENSION

*Read the following three paragraphs. Pay attention to the underlined words.*

### Paragraph 1: Grizzly Bears

Grizzly bears are <u>native</u> to North America. In Alaska, there are still many <u>wild</u> grizzly bears. But there aren't many left in other parts of North America because people have killed so many of them. <u>Hunters</u> kill bears because they want the bears' fur and meat. Other people, such as farmers, kill bears because they want to <u>protect</u> their farm animals and their families.

### Paragraph 2: The Ivory Problem

Sarah's grandmother gave her a beautiful set of ten knives and forks with <u>ivory</u> handles for her wedding. Sarah could not accept the gift because she knew that hunters have to kill elephants to get ivory. She <u>convinced</u> her grandmother that it was wrong to buy ivory, so her grandmother took back the gift and made a <u>donation</u> to Save the Elephants Fund.

**Paragraph 3: Logging in the United States**

In the 1800s in the United States, <u>loggers</u> used to cut down trees wherever they wanted, and people cut down woods and forests so that they could build houses and farms. <u>By 1907</u>, almost 30 percent (286 million acres) of the United States's forests were gone. So the government decided it needed to <u>protect</u> the forests and it made some new laws. Now it is <u>illegal</u> to cut down trees in many places.

*Now write the words next to their correct definitions.*

| by 1907 | donation | illegal | loggers | protect |
|---------|----------|---------|---------|---------|
| convince | hunter | ivory | native | wild |

1. _____: to keep someone or something safe

2. _____: no later than that time

3. _____: a gift (usually money) to an organization

4. _____: someone who kills animals, usually for food

5. _____: bone-like material that comes from elephant tusks; in the past, was often used to make jewelry

6. _____: people who cut down trees to use the wood

7. _____: in nature; not in a house or a zoo

8. _____: born in a certain place

9. _____: against the law

10. _____: to change someone's opinion about something

tusk

# 2 Focus on Reading

*Read the title and the first paragraph of the letter. Then answer these questions.*

**1.** Who is the letter to? Who is the letter from?

**2.** What do you think the writer of the letter wants?

*Now read the rest of the letter. Were your guesses correct?*

## SAVE THE ELEPHANTS FUND
2354 Massachusetts Avenue, NW
Washington, D.C. 01012

October 14, 2004

Dear Friend of SAVE THE ELEPHANTS FUND,

1     Thank you for your generous donation last year. Your money helped us to open a new wildlife park[1] in Kenya as part of our work to help protect the 500,000 elephants left in Africa.

2     Unfortunately, elephants are endangered in other parts of the world, too, and we need your help again. This time we need you to help us in Thailand.

3     One hundred years ago, millions of wild elephants lived in Asia. Today there are only 30,000 Asian elephants. The situation in Thailand is especially serious. Thailand now has only 1,800 to 2,000 elephants. Experts believe that by the year 2010, elephants in Thailand will be extinct.

---

[1] *wildlife park:* a park for wild animals where it is illegal to kill the animals.

4    **Why are elephants in Thailand endangered?**

5    • They don't have enough food to eat.

Paper companies cut down banana trees and bamboo. These plants are native to Thailand, and they are eaten by elephants. The companies plant eucalyptus trees instead. The eucalyptus trees grow fast, and the companies use their wood for boxes and other paper products. The paper companies make a lot of money from the eucalyptus trees. But what about the elephants? They need 150 to 300 kilograms of food every day, and they can't eat eucalyptus trees!

6    • Hunters kill hundreds of wild elephants every year.

Hunting elephants is not legal in Thailand, but many hunters kill these animals anyway. These illegal hunters make a lot of money from selling elephant tusks. The only way to get the tusk off the elephant is to kill the animal. The hunters sell the tusks to people who make furniture, jewelry, and art from the ivory in the tusks.

7    **What can we do?**

8    With your help and donation, this year we will:

• teach companies in Thailand about trees that are good for business and good for elephants

• pay for game wardens[2] to protect the elephants from illegal hunting

• convince people around the world not to buy things made of ivory

• help hunters to find other ways to make money

9    Last year you helped Kenya's elephants. This year Thailand's elephants need your help. Please send your donation today.

Thank you.


Sincerely,

*Mark Gow*

Mark Gow

Executive Director

## READING FOR MAIN IDEAS

*Work with a partner. Answer the following questions. Write your answers.*

1. What is the general purpose of Save the Elephants Fund?

   _____

2. Why are elephants in Thailand endangered?

   _____

   _____

3. What can Save the Elephants Fund do to help protect elephants in Thailand? *(List two possibilities.)*

   _____

   _____


## READING FOR DETAILS

*Read each statement. Decide if it is true or false. Write **T** (true) or **F** (false) next to it. Compare your answers with a classmate's.*

_____ 1. Last year Save the Elephants Fund used donations to open a wildlife park in Kenya.

_____ 2. There are more than 2,000 wild elephants in Thailand now.

_____ 3. Paper companies in Thailand find banana trees useful for boxes and other paper products.

_____ 4. In Thailand, it is illegal to hunt elephants.

_____ 5. Save the Elephants Fund wants the paper companies to leave Thailand.

_____ 6. Save the Elephants Fund wants to help hunters in Thailand to find other jobs.


## REACTING TO THE READING

**1** *Answer the questions. Compare your answers with a classmate's.*

1. Does the writer of the letter know the reader? How do you know?

   _____

2. The letter says, "we need your help." What does that mean? What kind of help does Save the Elephants Fund want?

   _____

**3.** Why does Save the Elephants Fund tell the reader how many elephants there are in Thailand today?

_____

**4.** Save the Elephants Fund says it wants to convince people not to buy ivory. How does this help save elephants?

_____

_____

**5.** Save the Elephants Fund says it will "help hunters find other ways to make money." How does this help save elephants?

_____

_____

**2** _Check (✓) the statement that best describes your opinion. Then compare and discuss your answers in groups of three or four._

_____ **1.** It is very important for people in the United States to help save the elephants in Thailand.

_____ **2.** It is more important for people in the United States to help to save endangered animals in the United States.

_____ **3.** It is more important for people in the United States to help the people in Thailand and other countries.

_____ **4.** People in the United States should help to save elephants, but they should also remember to help other animals and people all over the world.

## B  READING TWO: *Save a Logger—Eat an Owl*

*Read the following letter to the editor of a newspaper. It is a response to an article about the northern spotted owl.*

**To the Editor  •  To the Editor  •  To the Editor  •  To the Editor**

### Save a Logger—Eat an Owl

1    I am really angry about the article on the northern spotted owl. The article talked only about saving the owl. But what about us—the loggers?

2    The town I live in was built on logging. In the early 1980s, we cut 86 million feet of wood each year. That is a lot of wood. A lot of wood meant a lot of jobs—and a lot of money for the town. This money kept our schools open and our local government running. But by 1992, we were cutting only 100,000 feet of wood a year. Why? Because people like you who just care about the owls stopped us from doing our jobs. You convinced the government to stop logging companies from cutting down so many trees. As a result, over 30,000 logging jobs have been lost. Some people have moved away to find work. Others stayed here and took jobs that pay half of what they made as loggers. People have a hard time putting food on the table for their families. Our schools have no money. Our town is a third of the size that it used to be.

3    I'm not against the spotted owl, but saving the owl is hurting people. What is more important—a few owls or the lives of thousands of hardworking families?

*Ken Waxter, Oregon*

*Now, in a small group, discuss the following questions.*

1. Why is Ken Waxter angry?

2. Why did the logging companies in Ken's town stop cutting down so many trees?

3. How does saving the northern spotted owl hurt Ken Waxter and other people in his town?

## C  LINKING READINGS ONE AND TWO

*Work in a small group. Complete the following chart. Use information from Readings One and Two. Share your answers with the class.*

|  | Asian Elephants | Northern Spotted Owls |
|---|---|---|
| **1.** Why are the animals endangered? | | |
| **2.** What can people do to help save these animals? | | |
| **3.** Who might be hurt when people try to save the animals? Why? | | |

*Using the information in the chart, discuss these questions with the class.*

1. Name some other animals that are endangered now. What kinds of things can people do to save them?

2. What kinds of problems happen when people try to save endangered animals?

# 3 Focus on Vocabulary

**1** *Cross out the word or phrase that is not related to the boldfaced word.*

1. **protect:** save, fix, watch

2. **wild:** tigers, dogs, whales

3. **donation:** animals, money, help

4. **ivory:** white, bird, elephant

5. **hunter:** guns, plants, animals

6. **native:** of the place, born in the place, brought into the place

7. **by the year 2010:** between now and 2010, before 2010, in 2010

8. **convince:** talk to, change someone's mind, get angry

9. **illegal:** police, saving, wrong

10. **logger:** animals, trees, worker

**2** *Look at the following letter from Save the Dolphins. Complete the sentences using the words in the list below. Three of the words are not used.*

| by the year | donation | illegal | logger | protect |
| convince | hunter | ivory | native | wild |

# SAVE THE DOLPHINS
**1452 Battery St., Suite 200**
**San Francisco, CA 94111**

January 17, 2004

Dear Friend of the Dolphin,

    Chinese white dolphins are (1) _____ to the area near Hong Kong. They are endangered because the water near Hong Kong is becoming very dirty. If we don't (2) _____ these dolphins, they might become extinct (3) _____ 2020.

    We need to (4) _____ companies to stop putting chemicals and garbage in the water. We are also working to make it (5) _____ to catch the Chinese white dolphins and put them in aquariums. Dolphins are (6) _____ animals—they never live very long in aquariums.

    Your (7) _____ will help us start a Hong Kong Harbor water cleanup project. Please send a check today so that we can save the Chinese white dolphins.

            Sincerely,

            *Jon Jackson*

            Jon Jackson

            President, Save the Dolphins

**3** *Read the description of Sarah's situation, then finish Sarah's letter for her. Use information that you have learned in this unit. Use at least eight of the new vocabulary words listed below. The letter has been started for you.*

Sarah is getting married. She and her future husband are very active in Save the Elephants Fund. Sarah just received a wedding gift of ivory-handled knives and forks from her grandmother. She is writing a letter to her grandmother to tell her why she cannot accept the gift.

| | | | | | |
|---|---|---|---|---|---|
| convince | endangered | hunter | ivory | protect | wild |
| donation | extinct | illegal | logger | save | |

---

May 30, 2004

Dear Grandma,

    The wedding gift you sent is really beautiful. You are very kind, but I cannot accept this gift. I wanted to write this letter to tell you why. I hope that you understand.

    The knives and forks have handles made of ivory. _____

_____

_____

_____

_____

_____

_____

I love you,
Sarah

---

# 4 Focus on Writing

## A  STYLE: Letter Writing

**1** *Letters have five parts: date, opening, body, closing, and signature. Read the letter to Julie from Christine. Try to label the five parts of this letter.*

September 30, 2004

Dear Julie,

Hi! Thanks for your letter. Your vacation plans sound like so much fun!

What interests you about Kenya? I am interested in going to Africa too. I hear that the animals in Kenya are amazing. I'd like to know more about your trip and the tour group. Who leads the tours? Where do the guests sleep? If you sleep in tents, I think I will find another tour group! I would be too scared of having an elephant walk over me while I sleep.

What do you need to bring? I have an old suitcase, but maybe I should buy a backpack. How much does the trip cost? When do you need to pay? I don't have much money in the bank right now, but I guess I could use a credit card. Who do I call if I am interested in going?

By the way, why do you want to go in December? Isn't it really hot there at that time of year?

I'll call you soon to talk more about the trip. Maybe we can go together.

All the best,
Christine

## The Five Parts of a Letter

The letter from Christine is a **personal letter** from one friend to another. Like all letters, it has five parts:

1. **Date:** usually in the top right corner of the paper

2. **Opening:** a greeting to the person you are writing to—"Dear," the person's name, and a comma

3. **Body:** your message—one or more paragraphs

4. **Closing:** a word or phrase (like "All the best," "Best wishes," or "Yours truly") followed by a comma

5. **Signature:** your first name only for people you know; your full name for other people

The letter on pages 61–62 from Save the Elephants Fund is a **business letter.** A business letter has the same five parts as a personal letter, but there are a few differences.

In a business letter, usually:

- Your **name and address** come after the date. (The name and address of Save the Elephants Fund comes at the top of the page because it is already printed on the paper. This kind of printed name and address is called *letterhead.* Most businesses use letterheads on their letters.)

- If you are writing to a specific person, the name, title, and address of that person comes next, before the opening.

- If you do not know who will read your letter, for the **opening** write "To Whom It May Concern."

- Use "Sincerely," for the **closing.**

- Your name (printed if you are not typing) and job title (if you have one) go under your **signature.**

- Business letters should be typed, if possible.

**2** *Label the five parts of the letter from Save the Dolphins on page 67.*

**3** *Save the Elephants Fund received a large donation from Robin Tucci. Mark Gow must write a letter thanking Robin Tucci for her donation. Write a business letter for him, using the information below. Be sure to include all five parts of a letter.*

TO:         Robin Tucci

ADDRESS:    5325 Sylvan Avenue
            Oakland, CA 94618

FROM:       Mark Gow, Executive Director

ADDRESS:    Save the Elephants Fund
            2354 Massachusetts Avenue, NW
            Washington, D.C. 01012

DATE:       Use today's date.

MESSAGE:    Thank you for your kind donation of $1,000.00. Your money helps
            us work to save the elephants in Thailand and other parts of the
            world. Our fund could not carry out this important work without
            the support of generous people like you. Thanks again.

## B    GRAMMAR: *Wh–* Questions in the Simple Present Tense

**1** *Read these questions from the letter on page 69. Look at the verbs in the questions. What is the difference between the verbs in column A and those in column B?*

**Column A**

Where <u>do</u> the guests <u>sleep</u>?
What <u>do</u> you <u>need</u> to bring?
When <u>do</u> you <u>need</u> to pay?
Who <u>do</u> I <u>call</u> if I am interested in going?
Why <u>do</u> you <u>want</u> to go in December?

**Column B**

What <u>interests</u> you about Kenya?
Who <u>leads</u> the tours?

### *Wh–* Questions in the Simple Present Tense

**1.** *Wh–* questions ask for **information.** They cannot be answered by *yes* or *no.*

   A: **What** do I need?

   B: You need a backpack.

*Wh–* questions start with a *wh–* word like ***what, where, when, who,*** and ***why.***

*(continued)*

**2.** To form **most *wh*– questions** in the simple present tense, use **do** or **does** and the base form of the verb.

| *Wh*– Word | *Do/Does* | Subject | Base Form | |
|---|---|---|---|---|
| **Where** | **do** | the guests | **sleep?** | |
| **Why** | **does** | she | **want** | to go in December? |
| **Who** | **do** | I | **call** | if I am interested in going? |

EXCEPTION: With the verb **be,** do not use *do* or *does*.

| **Where** | **are** | the elephants? |
|---|---|---|
| **Who** | **is** | he? |

**3.** To form ***wh*- questions about the subject** of a sentence, do not use *do* and *does*. Use the third-person singular form of the verb.

| Subject (*Who, What*) | Third-Person Singular Form of Verb | |
|---|---|---|
| **Who** | **leads** | the tours? |
| **What** | **interests** | you about Kenya? |

**2** *Read each sentence. Write a question that the underlined words can answer.*

**1.** Pandas live <u>in China</u>.

  *Where do pandas live?* _____

**2.** <u>Chinese white dolphins</u> live in the water near Hong Kong.

  _____

**3.** The Chinese white dolphins die <u>because their water is dirty</u>.

  _____

**4.** Elephants in Thailand like to eat <u>native trees</u>.

  _____

**5.** Game wardens protect the elephants <u>in the daytime and at night</u>.

  _____

**6.** <u>Hunters</u> kill many endangered animals every year.

  _____

**3** *Michele works for Save the Elephants Fund, and she is calling Mrs. Jewell. Fill in the missing questions. Use Michele's answers to write the correct questions.*

MRS. JEWELL:  Hello?

MICHELE:  Hi. My name is Michele. I'm calling from the Save the Elephants Fund. Do you have a minute?

MRS. JEWELL:  Sure. Tell me again, (1) who *do you work for* ?

MICHELE:  I work for Save the Elephants Fund. We try to save endangered elephants in many different countries. This year we're working in Thailand.

MRS. JEWELL:  I thought there were a lot of elephants in Thailand. (2) Why _____ ?

MICHELE:  We need to save them because they're endangered. There are actually only about 2,000 wild elephants in Thailand now. They're endangered because people kill them and . . .

MRS. JEWELL:  Oh, no! (3) Who _____ ?

MICHELE:  Elephant hunters kill them.

MRS. JEWELL:  Really? (4) Why _____ ?

MICHELE:  Because they want to sell the ivory from the elephants' tusks.

MRS. JEWELL:  That's terrible! What can you do about it? How can I help?

MICHELE:  Well, you can send us a donation.

MRS. JEWELL:  OK. (5) Where _____ ?

MICHELE:  You send it to 2354 Massachusetts Avenue, NW, Washington, D.C. 01012.

MRS. JEWELL:  (6) Who _____ ?

MICHELE:  You write the check to "Save the Elephants Fund." Thank you very much for your donation!

MRS. JEWELL:  Oh, you're welcome, and good luck.

# C  WRITING TOPICS

*Choose one of the following topics. Write one paragraph. Use some of the vocabulary, grammar, and style that you learned in this unit.*

1. You have $300 to donate to one of the groups from Section 1C, pages 58–59, but you have some questions. Write a letter to one of the groups. Say that you want to help, but you want to ask some questions first. Ask at least three *wh-* questions. Remember to include all five parts of a letter.

2. You have $300 to donate. Will you give your money to Save the Elephants Fund? Why or why not? Give as many reasons as you can.

3. What are some endangered animals you know about? Do you think it is important to save these and other endangered animals? Why or why not?

4. There are several bumper stickers about saving or not saving endangered animals. Look at the ones below. Which bumper sticker do you agree with? Explain your answer.

# D  RESEARCH TOPIC

*Work in small groups. Write a letter asking for help for an endangered animal. Follow these steps.*

1. Choose an endangered animal.

2. Get information about this animal from the library or the Internet. The information should help you answer the following questions:

   a. Why is this animal endangered? (*at least two reasons*)

   b. What can people do to save this animal? (*at least two ideas*)

   c. What groups (like Save the Elephants Fund or Friends of the Tiger) help protect this animal?

3. Write the letter. Address it to the other students in your school ("Dear Fellow Students,"). Explain to them:

a. why this animal is endangered

b. how they can contact a group to learn more about the problem

c. how they can help

Remember to include the five parts of a letter. Have everyone in your group sign it.

4. Share your letter with another group. Read the other group's letter. Then answer these questions:

a. Did the writers include the five parts of a letter?

b. If the writers used *wh-* questions, did they use them correctly? Underline any verb you think might be incorrect. Talk it over with the other group.

c. Is there a sentence you do not understand? Underline it. Ask the other group to explain it to you.

For step-by-step practice in the writing process, see the *Writing Activity Book, Basic/Low Intermediate, Second Edition,* Unit 4.

| | |
|---|---|
| Assignment: | Writing a Persuasive Letter |
| Prewriting: | Brainstorming |
| Organizing: | Persuading the Reader |
| Revising: | Explaining Reasons; Asking *Wh–* Questions |
| Editing: | Formatting a Letter |

For Unit 4 Internet activities, visit the NorthStar Companion Website at http://www.longman.com/northstar.

UNIT **5**

# "Netiquette"

# 1 Focus on the Topic

## A PREDICTING

Look at the picture, and discuss these questions with the class.

1. What are the people doing?

2. Can you tell how each person feels?

3. When these symbols[1] are used in an e-mail, what do they communicate?

   :)     :))     :D     :O     >:(     :(

4. Read the title of the unit. What do you think it means?

---

[1] To understand these symbols (called "emoticons"), tilt your head to the left.

# B   SHARING INFORMATION

*Work in a group of four students. Write the names of each student in the group at the top of the chart. Discuss the questions in the chart, and write each student's answers.*

| Questions | name | name | name | name |
|---|---|---|---|---|
| **1.** Do you have an e-mail address? | | | | |
| **2.** Who do you e-mail most? (family, friends, co-workers) | | | | |
| **3.** What do you like best about e-mail? | | | | |
| **4.** What are some problems with e-mail? | | | | |
| **5.** How often do you write letters using "snail mail" or the regular postal system? | | | | |

*Now each group reports to the class.*

**Example:**  In our group, two people have an e-mail address, and two do not.

# C  PREPARING TO READ

## BACKGROUND

*Look at the graph. Then answer the questions below.*

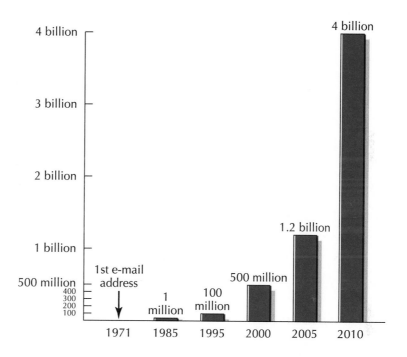

**Number of E-mail Addresses Worldwide**

1. When did e-mail start?

   _____

2. When were there only 1 million e-mail addresses?

   _____

3. How many e-mail addresses were there in 2000?

   _____

4. How many e-mail addresses will there be in 2010?

   _____

## VOCABULARY FOR COMPREHENSION

*Read the sentences. Pay attention to the underlined words.*

**a.** Sally likes to be <u>calm</u> in the morning. She usually sits in the kitchen by herself for an hour, quietly reading the newspaper.

**b.** When she heard about her mother's illness, Andy got very <u>upset</u>.

**c.** Julia never says please or thank you. She is <u>rude</u>.

**d.** Diego always says please and thank you. He is <u>polite</u>.

**e.** Yesterday I got a letter from an old school friend. I wrote a letter back to him right away. I always <u>reply</u> quickly to my friends.

**f.** I can never find the CD I'm looking for. I have too many CDs to look through. Someday I'm going to <u>organize</u> my CDs.

**g.** I could see that she didn't feel comfortable talking about her family. I wanted to change the <u>subject</u>. So I asked her questions about her job.

**h.** Maya gets a lot of e-mail. She <u>receives</u> 30 messages a day.

**i.** My mother and her brother had a fight a long time ago. They stopped seeing each other, talking to each other, or even writing to each other. They didn't <u>communicate</u> for 15 years.

**j.** Please don't read this journal. It's <u>private</u>. This is where I write all my special thoughts and ideas. I don't want anyone to read it.

*Now use the words to complete the definitions.*

1. To _____ is to talk, write, or otherwise contact another person.

2. Something is _____ when it is not shared with anyone else.

3. To be _____ is to be peaceful, not angry or upset.

4. The _____ of a story is the main idea or topic.

5. To _____ is to get something that someone has sent you.

6. To _____ is to plan or arrange something.

7. To be _____ is to say or do things that are not nice or polite.

8. To be _____ is to say or do things that are nice and respectful.

9. To _____ is to send an answer to a letter or e-mail.

10. To be _____ is to be unhappy or worried.

# 2 Focus on Reading

## A  READING ONE: *"Netiquette" Do's and Don'ts*

*The following article is taken from an online newsletter for banking employees. Read the title and the introduction. Then answer these questions.*

**1.** What is "netiquette"?

**2.** Why do people need to know about "netiquette"?

*Now read the article. Were your ideas correct?*

### "Netiquette" Do's and Don'ts

**By Sarah Byrne**

For many people all over the world, e-mail is the best way of communicating quickly, cheaply, and easily. Because it is so fast and easy, it is also very easy to *miscommunicate.* To send clear, easy-to-understand e-mails, follow these basic rules of e-mail use—called network etiquette, or "netiquette."

**Netiquette Do's**

1. ☺: Keep your e-mails short. Separate your ideas into different paragraphs. Some people receive hundreds of e-mails a day. They hate reading through long messages. They want to receive short, easy-to-read messages.

2. ☺: Check your message before you send it. Make sure it says what you want it to say. Remember that you are writing, not talking. For example, how can you show in writing that you are joking? One way is to use "emoticons." These are pictures made with punctuation marks, like :) . The colon is the two eyes and the parenthesis is the mouth.

3. ☺: Check your spelling. There is no reason for poor spelling, even in e-mail.

4. ☺: Fill in the subject for each e-mail. This helps people organize e-mails and find old ones. Also, if someone has hundreds of e-mails to read, he or she might not read one without a subject, just to save time.

5. ☺: Include your "signature" at the end of every message. Every message should include your signature because it is not always clear who sent an e-mail. An e-mail signature includes your full name, e-mail address, and often your "snail mail" or street address and telephone number.

**Netiquette Don'ts**

6. ☹: Don't use all capital letters. This is the same as SHOUTING. It is rude.

7. ☹: Don't send everyone a copy when you only want to send a message to one person. Often we are sent messages as a "cc" (carbon copy—the old word for a copy of a letter). When we reply to these messages, we have to be very careful to reply only to the person we want to read our message.

8. ☹: Don't send e-mails when you are angry or upset. These messages are called "flames." Wait until you are calm to reply. Also, don't send e-mails that will get you flamed. Be polite and try not to make anyone angry or upset.

9. ☹: Don't think e-mail is private. E-mail is written communication. Never write something in an e-mail that you wouldn't say in public.

There are a lot of things to think about when writing e-mail, but following these rules will help you to communicate clearly. Happy e-mailing!

## READING FOR MAIN IDEAS

*Check (✓) the phrase that best completes the main idea of Reading One.*

Following e-mail etiquette rules will help you _____.

_____  **a.** communicate clearly and correctly

_____  **b.** express your emotions

_____  **c.** make sure the right person or people read your message

## READING FOR DETAILS

*The statements below are false. Correct them to make true statements that summarize each of the nine rules given in Reading One.*

          *short*
1. Keep your e-mails ~~long~~.

2. Don't read your message before you send it.

3. Don't check your English.

4. Don't write the subject of each e-mail.

5. Don't include a signature with every e-mail.

6. Don't use capital letters.

7. Don't send anyone a copy of every message.

8. Don't send e-mails when you feel relaxed.

9. Write very private things in e-mail.

**REACTING TO THE READING**

**1** *Read the following statements. Check (✓) those statements that you think are supported by information in Reading One.*

_____ **1.** Short e-mails are easier to read than long e-mails.

_____ **2.** Sending messages in writing is clearer than in speaking.

_____ **3.** People make more spelling mistakes in e-mail than in ordinary letters.

_____ **4.** What you write in the subject line must be the main idea of the e-mail.

_____ **5.** Most people don't include their signatures.

_____ **6.** Sending e-mails when you are angry could get you "flamed."

_____ **7.** Most people use e-mail to communicate with friends.

**2** *Discuss the following questions in a small group. Give your opinions.*

**1.** Which netiquette rules do you follow? Which of these rules are new to you?

**2.** Do you think it's a good idea for everyone to follow all of these rules? Some of these rules? Explain.

**3.** Have you ever made a netiquette "mistake"? If yes, describe what happened.

**B** **READING TWO:** *Dear Debbie*

*Read this excerpt from a newspaper advice column called "Dear Debbie."*

# Dear Debbie

E-mail. Everyone's doing it. It's so fast. It's made communicating with each other so easy. But there's a dark side to e-mail. Recently, I've received a lot of letters from people in big trouble caused by the e-mail "blooper" (mistake). Read on to see what kinds of trouble the e-mail blooper can make.

Dear Debbie,
Help! Last week, I received an e-mail message from my best friend at work. It was a general message about the holiday party sent to the whole company. I wrote back to my friend saying that I wasn't going to the party. Then, I went on to tell

her how much I hated working at this company. I told her how I thought my other co-workers were stupid and boring. I explained how I thought our boss was not nice and treated us all badly. I meant to hit the REPLY button to send my friend the e-mail. Instead, I hit the REPLY ALL button which sent the message to my best friend, all ten co-workers, and my boss! Everything I wrote in the e-mail is true. But I would never say those things to my boss or other co-workers. I was so embarrassed, I took a few days off from work pretending to be sick. I just couldn't face all these people. But I have to go back to work soon. What do I say to them?

*Embarrassed in Emeryville*

**Dear Debbie,**
What can I do? Recently, a longtime friend made me very upset. We live far apart, so I wanted to write a very organized, thoughtful e-mail explaining how I felt. I planned to write two drafts of the e-mail. In my first draft, I just wrote everything I was feeling. I was very angry, and at that moment, I felt that everything about her and our friendship was wrong. I wrote all this in the message. I then saved the e-mail and went on to other things, planning to rewrite it later, when I was less upset.

You can see what's coming. Somehow, when working on another e-mail, I clicked SEND and accidentally sent this first draft of the e-mail to my friend. Of course, she is now so angry. She thinks I'm a terrible friend to send such a message to her. What can I say to her?

*Sorry in Cincinnati*

**Dear Debbie,**
My wife and I are having an argument. We share a computer and the other day she was looking in the "trash" for an old file she had thrown out. While she was looking around for her lost file, she found all these old e-mails of mine sent to an ex-girlfriend. You see, my wife is not happy about me keeping in touch with this old girlfriend. So, I've been secretly e-mailing her for years. It's nothing really. But because I know it would make my wife mad, I've been careful to delete the messages. Well, I thought I was deleting the messages. I guess they were just sent to the "trash." I didn't know I had to "empty the trash" to really get rid of them. Anyway, my wife read them and is now really mad at me. She says I should apologize[1] for writing to my ex-girlfriend. I say I haven't done anything wrong. In fact, I think she should apologize for reading e-mails not sent to her. Who's right?

*Mad in Miami*

---

[1] *apologize:* to say you're sorry.

---

*Now discuss the following questions in a small group.*

**1.** In the first letter, why did *Embarrassed in Emeryville* send that e-mail to everyone in his office?

_____

**2.** In the second letter, who was *Sorry in Cincinnati* trying to send e-mails to?

_____

**3.** In the third letter, why is *Mad in Miami's* wife angry?

_____

## C   LINKING READINGS ONE AND TWO

**1** *Reread the netiquette rules from Reading One. Which rule did each e-mail blooper break? Write your answers below. Then discuss your answers with a partner.*

E-mail blooper 1: _____

E-mail blooper 2: _____

E-mail blooper 3: _____

**2** *Pretend you are an assistant to Debbie. She asks you to help her write responses to these letters.*

*Choose one of the three e-mail bloopers, and fill in the following letter outline with the appropriate information. Use what you know of netiquette rules from Reading One to help you.*

```
Dear _____,


   As I see it, there are two problems. One is the e-mail

problem. How can you prevent this mistake from happening

again? Remember, when using e-mail, always _____

_____

_____.



   The second problem is more difficult. How do you fix the

problem your e-mail mistake caused? In your case, I think

you should _____

_____.

I think you should do this because _____

_____.



   Good luck, and remember to be more careful with your

e-mail next time.


Debbie
```

# 3 Focus on Vocabulary

**1** *What is a prefix? Read the following presentation.*

> A **prefix** is a group of letters that can be added at the beginning of a word to change the meaning of the word. Sometimes knowing a prefix can help you guess the meaning of unfamiliar words.

*Now read this excerpt from Reading One. Notice the underlined words. Answer the questions below.*

> For many people all over the world, e-mail is the best way of <u>communicating</u> quickly, cheaply, and easily. Because it is so fast and easy, it is also very easy to <u>miscommunicate</u>. To send clear, easy-to-understand e-mails, follow these basic rules of e-mail use—called network etiquette or "netiquette."

**1.** What is the difference between the two words?

_____

**2.** The prefix *mis-* appears in *misunderstand, misuse,* and *misplace.* Guess the meaning of the prefix *mis-*.

_____

**2** *Work with a partner. Read each group of sentences. Notice the underlined words. All have the same prefix. Guess the meaning of the prefix and write it on the line.*

**1.** *un-* means _____
   **a.** Most doctors agree that potato chips are <u>unhealthy</u> for you. They suggest you eat healthy snacks like fruits and vegetables.
   **b.** Why are these bills still <u>unpaid</u>? Don't we have enough money in our checking account?
   **c.** She is so <u>unhappy</u>. She just found out that she didn't do well on the last exam.

**2.** *tri-* means _____
   **a.** I was so excited when I could finally ride a bicycle instead of <u>tricycle</u>.
   **b.** In my classroom in Los Angeles, 15 of the children are bilingual—they speak English and Spanish. One student is <u>trilingual</u> in Chinese, Vietnamese, and English.
   **c.** Squares have four sides and four corners. <u>Triangles</u> have three sides and three corners.

**3.** *co-* means _____
   **a.** I work with a lot of different people. My co-workers come from ten different countries.
   **b.** In most big airplanes there are two people who fly the plane: the pilot and the co-pilot.
   **c.** We need to learn to work together. We need to cooperate.

**4.** *re-* means _____
   **a.** You have a test tomorrow. So let's review all the new vocabulary words we learned this week.
   **b.** The library is closed for repairs. It will re-open next week at the regularly scheduled time.
   **c.** My teacher says my essay is OK. She thinks if I rewrite it, it'll be much better.

**3** *Complete the sentences with the correct prefix for each underlined word.*

| co- | mis- | re- | tri- | un- |
| --- | --- | --- | --- | --- |

1. I'm sorry. Can you repeat that? I think I _____ understood you.

2. He hurt his back in a skiing accident. He is _____ able to ski or lift heavy things anymore.

3. I've read the directions once, but I still don't understand what I'm supposed to do. I guess I'll have to _____ read the directions.

4. They want to buy a house together. That way they will be _____ owners of the house.

5. I see a lot of mistakes in your essay. There are several grammar mistakes and you _____ spelled several important words.

6. To get a nice photograph, I rest my camera on a _____ pod. Its three feet make it strong and stable.

7. She was the nicest woman, but her husband was not. He was _____ friendly.

8. Our house burned down in the 1991 Oakland fire. It took five years for us to _____ build it.

**4** *Read the following information about the beginnings of e-mail.*

In 1968 a company called Bolt Beranek and Newman (BBN) was hired by the United States Defense Department to build Arpanet. Arpanet later became what we now call the Internet. In 1971, while working for BBN, an engineer named Ray Tomlinson developed the first system for sending e-mail between computers. In a recent e-mail interview, Ray Tomlinson wrote about his own experience with e-mail.

*Now read the interview and fill in the blanks with words from the box.*

| boring | embarrassed | polite | reply | subject |
| communicate | organize | received | rude | upset |

Q: *Ray, could you tell us about the very first e-mail?*

A: Well, the first e-mail was sent by myself to myself. I wrote it on one computer

and sent it to my other computer which was about 15 feet away. At the time,

I had no idea that e-mail would turn into such a big thing. Looking back

on it, I feel like I should have written some very important message. I'm

_____ to say that I don't remember what I wrote in that first
         1.

message.

Q: *I read that 9.8 billion messages are sent every day on e-mail. People use it at*

*work, to keep in touch with family and friends, to share information, to meet*

*each other. When did you first notice that this program you wrote had*

*changed the way people _____?*
                              2.

A: Well, to be honest, no one thought it was very interesting at the beginning.

I knew that I and my fellow computer programmers found e-mail very useful.

The rest of the world seemed to think it was quite _____, or at
                                                        3.

least not very interesting. But, around 1994 I got a lot of phone calls for

interviews about e-mail. Then, I realized what a big thing it was.

Q: *Everyone has a different e-mail writing style. What can you tell me about your e-mail style?*

A: I write very short e-mails. Sometimes people think I'm angry or

_____ because I write such short e-mails. For example,
⁴·

when someone has written me an e-mail with a lot of questions, I'll

_____ to each question and not write anything else. I know
⁵·

some people think this is _____ or not very nice. I want to be
⁶·

_____, but I also need to answer a lot of e-mails. So, I write
⁷·

short ones.

Q: *You must get a lot of e-mail every day. How much? How do you deal with it?*

A: I get quite a lot of e-mail. For example, yesterday, I sent 14 messages and

_____ 150 messages. I get so many messages that sometimes
⁸·

I don't read the whole message, I just read the _____ line to
⁹·

get a main idea of the message. Right now, I'm having trouble finding old

messages. I need to _____ my old e-mails better so I can go
¹⁰·

back and find old ones when I need them.

**5** *A friend who is doing a research project on e-mail use has sent you the following e-mail survey. Read it carefully before you reply (see page 91).*

---

**Research Project**

| | |
|---|---|
| **From:** | Margaret Ewing |
| **To:** | *(your e-mail address)* |
| **Sent:** | 9.10.04 |
| **Subject:** | Research Project |

Dear Friends,

I'm hoping you can help me with a research project I'm doing on e-mail use by ESL/EFL students.

Please respond to each of the questions below about your e-mail and Internet use. I will send you the results of my survey. Thank you very much.

Survey:

1. How many e-mails do you get each week? How many do you answer?

2. What language do you use most in your e-mails?

3. What are the most important things to remember when sending e-mails?

4. What do you do when someone "flames" you, or sends you an angry e-mail?

5. Has anything interesting happened to you as a result of e-mail?

Thanks for your help with my project.

Margaret Ewing
mewing@bullseye.com
43 Atwick Road
Baltimore, MD 21210
(410) 555–4515

*Now respond to each of Margaret's survey questions in an e-mail reply. Use at least one word from the box in each answer.*

| | | | | | |
|---|---|---|---|---|---|
| boring | communicate | organized | private | reply | subject |
| calm | embarrassed | polite | receive | rude | upset |

---

**Research Project**

**From:** _____

**To:** _____

**Sent:** _____

**Subject:** _____

Dear Margaret,

I got your message. Here are my answers to your survey questions.

1. _____

2. _____

3. _____

4. _____

5. _____

Good luck with your project. I look forward to learning the results of this survey.

_____

_____

_____

_____

_____

# 4 Focus on Writing

## A STYLE: Punctuation

**1** *Read this excerpt from Reading One. Circle all of the punctuation (periods, commas, etc.).*
*Then answer the questions that follow.*

> 2. ☺: Check your message before you send it. Make sure it says what you
> want it to say. Remember that you are writing, not talking. For example, how
> can you show in writing that you are joking? One way is to use "emoticons."
> These are pictures made with punctuation marks, like :) . The colon is the
> two eyes and the parenthesis is the mouth.

**1.** How many different kinds of punctuation did you find?

**2.** What is each kind of punctuation used for?

### Punctuation

**1.    .    period**

| | |
|---|---|
| Use a period to end a sentence that is a statement. | Check your message before you send it**.** |
| When you use a period as part of a number, call it *point*. | **5.5** (*five point five*) million messages are sent every hour. |

**2.    ,    comma**

| | |
|---|---|
| Commas are used for many different reasons, usually to separate parts of a sentence. | Remember that you are writing**,** not talking. |
| One of the most common uses is to separate short items in a list. | People use e-mail to communicate with families**,** friends**,** and co-workers. |
| We also use commas to help us read numbers that are larger than 999. Commas go in front of every third digit from the right. | By 2005**,** scientists guess that 1,200,000,000 people will use e-mail regularly. |

**3.    ?        question mark**

Use a question mark to end a question.

How can you show in writing that you are joking**?**

**4.    :        colon**

A colon sometimes introduces a list, especially if the list has long items.

Most e-mail programs offer lots of tools, which include**:**  reply buttons, spell check, attachment capability, address books, and cc buttons.

**5.    ;        semicolon**

A semicolon can be used instead of a period if two statements are very closely related.

In 1971, Ray Tomlinson wrote the first e-mail message**;** by 2001, 9.8 billion e-mail messages were being sent a day.

**6.    " "        quotation marks**

Quotation marks are used to report exactly what someone said.

Joe said, **"**Send me an e-mail on that.**"**

Quotation marks are also used around new words or expressions that the reader might not understand.

One way is to use what are called **"**emoticons.**"**

**7.    '        apostrophe**

Apostrophes are used to show possession.

Phoebe**'**s e-mail address isn**'**t easy to remember.

They are also used in contractions.

you will = **you'll**        do not = **don't**
is not = **isn't**

**8.    ()        parentheses**

Parentheses can go around information that helps explain something in a sentence but isn't needed to understand the sentence. For example, parentheses can go around definitions, background information, and examples.

Often we are sent messages as a cc **(**carbon copy—the old word for a copy of a letter**)**.

**9.    !        exclamation point**

Exclamation points are used at the end of sentences to show a lot of feeling.

Here's to happy e-mailing for all**!**

**2** *Put the correct punctuation in the blanks.*

1. 4 + 2.5 = 6 __ 5

2. 300 + 700 = 1 __ 000

3. What is your e-mail address __

4. I don't have an e-mail address __

5. Let me give you my phone number __ address __ and fax number.

6. A "flame" is an angry e-mail message __ "SPAM" is unwanted advertising e-mail messages __ "snail mail" is regular postal system mail.

7. She couldn't find his e-mail address. So she looked up his __ snail mail __ address __ his regular street address __ and wrote him a letter.

8. Tamara __ s boss doesn't like to use e-mail.

9. The equipment in our office includes __ faxes, computers, printers, copiers, video monitors, CD players, cassette players, and recording machines.

**3** *A student wrote the following paper and got it back from his teacher with comments. Rewrite the paper. Correct the punctuation. There are 15 mistakes.*

> Be careful with your punctuation.
>
> When I was a child in Thailand, I didn't write to my sisters brothers friends and parents. I just talked to them face to face. After I moved to the city, I called my friends and family on the telephone when I was lonely. Sometimes I'd call just to say, Hi. I miss you. I never wrote letters Then, in 1987, I moved to Los Angeles to study English. What could I do. I had to start writing. I wrote long letters to my family, but I didnt have time to write such long letters very often Also, the mail took a long time. Now, I write my family and friends using e-mail. I love it and its fast and much cheaper than a phone call and I can do it every day!
>
> This sentence seems very long. Can you separate your ideas?

## B   GRAMMAR:  Verbs Plus Gerunds and Infinitives

**1**  *Read this excerpt from Reading One. Notice the underlined words. Then answer the questions that follow.*

> 1. ☺: Keep your e-mails short. Separate your ideas into different paragraphs. Some people receive hundreds of e-mails a day. They <u>hate reading</u> through long messages. They <u>want to receive</u> short, easy-to-read messages.

**1.** What are the verbs? Circle them.

**2.** What word follows *hate*?

**3.** What words follow *want*?

**4.** What is different between the verb that follows *hate* and the verb that follows *want*?

### Verbs Plus Gerunds and Infinitives

**1.** Some verbs can be followed by a **gerund** (base form of the verb + *-ing*).
For example, *enjoy* and *keep*.

I ***enjoy searching*** the Internet for cheap airplane tickets.
She ***doesn't enjoy*** **writing** papers.

My father ***keeps refusing*** to buy a computer.

**2.** Some verbs can be followed by an **infinitive** (*to* + base form of the verb).
For example, *want* and *need*.

We ***want*** **to buy** a computer.
I ***don't want*** **to see** her.  I'll just send an e-mail.

People ***need*** **to be** careful when they make jokes in their e-mails.

**3.** Some verbs can be followed by **a gerund or an infinitive.**
For example, *like, love, hate, prefer.*

I ***like*** **talking** on the phone.
I ***like*** **to talk** on the phone.

I ***love*** **sending** e-mails sometimes, too.
I ***love*** **to send** e-mails sometimes, too.

**2** *Write sentences in the present tense, using the following words. Be sure to use the correct form of each verb.*

1. Marika / want / send / e-mail / to / her / sister.

_____

2. Timothy / not / like / write / letters / the / old-fashioned / way.

_____

3. Samantha / and / Pete / hate / use / computers / for / anything.

_____

4. Betsy / love / have / a / computer / to / help / her / with / drawing.

_____

5. Amanda / and / Wess / not / enjoy / receive / jokes / in / e-mails.

_____

6. I / need / get / a / computer / so / I / can / e-mail / my / sister / and / parents.

_____

7. You / prefer / use / the / telephone / instead / of / e-mail.

_____

8. My / parents / be / 70 / years / old, / but / they / love / use / a / computer.

_____

**3** *Work with a partner. Write a list of four sentences describing what e-mail writers need to do in order to write good e-mails.*

**Example**

*Writers need to make sure they send their messages to the correct people.*

1. _____

2. _____

3. _____

4. _____

**4** *Work in a small group. Discuss what you like and dislike about e-mail. Together at the board, write your ideas. Compare your ideas with other groups in the class.*

## C  WRITING TOPICS

*Choose one of the following topics. Write one paragraph. Use the information you learned in both Readings One and Two. Pay attention to gerunds and infinitives as well as punctuation.*

1. Follow the example of your response to a "Dear Debbie" letter on page 85. Write a response to one of the other "Dear Debbie" letters (pages 83–84).

2. Have you ever made an e-mail mistake that caused big trouble for you or someone else? Explain what happened.

3. A new co-worker has asked for your help. She is writing an e-mail to her boss and wants you to check it over before she sends it. Rewrite the following e-mail.

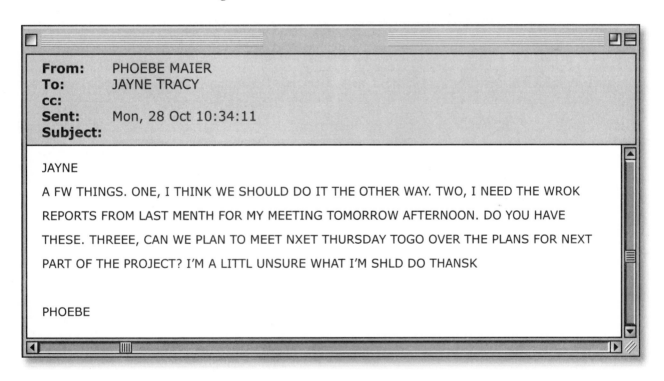

| | |
|---|---|
| **From:** | PHOEBE MAIER |
| **To:** | JAYNE TRACY |
| **cc:** | |
| **Sent:** | Mon, 28 Oct 10:34:11 |
| **Subject:** | |

JAYNE

A FW THINGS. ONE, I THINK WE SHOULD DO IT THE OTHER WAY. TWO, I NEED THE WROK

REPORTS FROM LAST MENTH FOR MY MEETING TOMORROW AFTERNOON. DO YOU HAVE

THESE. THREEE, CAN WE PLAN TO MEET NXET THURSDAY TOGO OVER THE PLANS FOR NEXT

PART OF THE PROJECT? I'M A LITTL UNSURE WHAT I'M SHLD DO THANSK

PHOEBE

4. In many offices around the world, e-mail is taking the place of quick face-to-face meetings or phone calls. Many office spaces, especially the open-plan office space, are quieter today than they were ten years ago, thanks to the use of office e-mail. What do you think of this change in the way people communicate at work? What are the advantages of using a lot of e-mail at work? What are some of the problems of communicating so much with e-mail?

# D RESEARCH TOPIC

The first e-mail was sent in 1971. Only recently have people started to use it in large numbers. It is still such a new way of communicating that there are no general rules to follow when using e-mail. As a result, most schools, universities, and large businesses have made their own e-mail rules, similar to the ones you read in Reading One. The rules described in Reading One are not the only rules, but they give you a good idea of what most places are trying to do.

*As a class, you will do a review of e-mails to see if people are following these rules of "netiquette." Which rules are followed? Which rules are broken?*

1. Work in a small group. Go into your e-mail archives or into an online chat room and select about ten short e-mails written in English. Read the e-mails together and decide which of the nine "netiquette" rules from Reading One are followed. Use the following chart to check (✓) those rules that are followed.

| E-mail | Rule 1 | Rule 2 | Rule 3 | Rule 4 | Rule 5 | Rule 6 | Rule 7 | Rule 8 | Rule 9 |
|--------|--------|--------|--------|--------|--------|--------|--------|--------|--------|
| 1 | | | | | | | | | |
| 2 | | | | | | | | | |
| 3 | | | | | | | | | |
| 4 | | | | | | | | | |
| 5 | | | | | | | | | |
| 6 | | | | | | | | | |
| 7 | | | | | | | | | |
| 8 | | | | | | | | | |
| 9 | | | | | | | | | |
| 10 | | | | | | | | | |

2. Share your results with another group. Tell them the following:

    **a.** which rules are followed the most frequently

    **b.** which are broken the most frequently

    **c.** which additional rules your group recommends

3. With your group, write a short paragraph, summarizing your research. In addition, write a new and improved list of e-mail etiquette rules that you and your group decided on.

4. Share your paragraph and your list with another group. Read the other group's paragraph and list. Then answer these questions:

    **a.** Did the writers use correct punctuation? Circle any incorrect punctuation.

    **b.** If the writers used gerunds and infinitives, did they use them correctly? Underline any verbs you think might be incorrect. Talk it over with the other group.

    **c.** Is there a rule you think is very interesting? Tell the other group why you think it is interesting.

---

For step-by-step practice in the writing process, see the *Writing Activity Book, Basic/Low Intermediate, Second Edition*, Unit 5.

| | |
|---|---|
| Assignment: | Writing a Paragraph about the Advantages and Disadvantages of Something |
| Prewriting: | Making a Tree Diagram |
| Organizing: | Giving Examples |
| Revising: | Developing Paragraph Unity |
| | Using Verbs Plus Gerunds and Infinitives |
| Editing: | Using Commas and Colons |

For Unit 5 Internet activities, visit the NorthStar Companion Website at http://www.longman.com/northstar.

# Women's Work?

# **1** Focus on the Topic

## A PREDICTING

Look at the advertisements for cleaning products from a magazine for women from the 1950s. Discuss these questions with the class.

1. What are the women in the ads doing?

2. How do you think they feel? Why?

3. Read the title of the unit. What do you think it means?

Advertisements from *Today's Woman*, September 1951, pp. 171, 174.

## B SHARING INFORMATION

*Who usually does the following chores in the home you live in now? Who usually did the chores in your home when you were growing up? Read the questions in the chart. Check (✓) your answers. Then compare answers with a classmate.*

| Chores | In Your Home Now | | | In Your Home When You Were Growing Up | | |
|---|---|---|---|---|---|---|
| | Usually Men | Sometimes Men, Sometimes Women | Usually Women | Usually Men | Sometimes Men, Sometimes Women | Usually Women |
| 1. Who washes the dishes? Who washed the dishes? | | | | | | |
| 2. Who takes out the garbage? Who took out the garbage? | | | | | | |
| 3. Who does the laundry? Who did the laundry? | | | | | | |
| 4. Who cleans the windows? Who cleaned the windows? | | | | | | |
| 5. Who dusts the furniture? Who dusted the furniture? | | | | | | |
| 6. Who vacuums? Who vacuumed? | | | | | | |

## C PREPARING TO READ

**BACKGROUND**

*Look at the chart. Read the sentences on page 103. Decide if the sentences are true or false. Write **T** (true) or **F** (false) next to each sentence.*

| Hours per Week Spent on Housework for American Women and Men | | |
|---|---|---|
| Year | Women | Men |
| 1950s | 30–35 | 6 |
| 1990s | 20–25 | 7 |

\_\_\_\_\_ **1.** In the 1950s, women did more housework than they did in the 1990s.

\_\_\_\_\_ **2.** In the 1990s, men did less housework than in the 1950s.

\_\_\_\_\_ **3.** In the 1990s, women and men did the same amount of housework.

\_\_\_\_\_ **4.** In the 1950s, women did more housework than men.

*Now discuss the chart in a small group. Is this information surprising? Is this the same in your home culture?*

## VOCABULARY FOR COMPREHENSION

*What do we use these cleaning products and tools for? Write the letter for each cleaning product or tool next to the phrase that tells what it is used for.*

\_\_\_\_\_ **1.** to clean the windows

\_\_\_\_\_ **2.** to dust the furniture

\_\_\_\_\_ **3.** to make clothes whiter

\_\_\_\_\_ **4.** to mop the floor

\_\_\_\_\_ **5.** to polish a silver cup

\_\_\_\_\_ **6.** to scrub a pot or skillet

\_\_\_\_\_ **7.** to scrub the tub or sink

\_\_\_\_\_ **8.** to wash clothes

\_\_\_\_\_ **9.** to wash dishes

\_\_\_\_\_ **10.** to wax the furniture

\_\_\_\_\_ **11.** to wipe the table

# 2 Focus on Reading

## A    READING ONE: *Housework*

*Look at the title of the following poem and read the first stanza (section or paragraph). Circle the types of housework that you think the poem will mention. You may also add more types of housework to the list.*

mowing the lawn             washing clothes             vacuuming the rugs

mopping the floors          washing the dishes          putting clothes away

_____            _____            _____

_____            _____            _____

*Now read the whole poem. Were your guesses correct?*

# Housework

## BY SHELDON HARNICK

1    1  You know, there are times when we happen to be
     2  just sitting there quietly watching TV,
     3  when the program we're watching will stop for
            awhile
     4  and suddenly someone appears with a smile
     5  and starts to show us how terribly urgent
            it is to buy some brand of detergent
            or soap or cleanser or cleaner or powder or paste or wax or bleach—
     6  to help with the housework.

2    7  Now, most of the time it's a lady we see who's doing the housework on the TV.
     8  She's cheerfully scouring[1] a skillet or two,
     9  or she's polishing pots 'til they gleam[2] like new,
     10 or she's scrubbing the tub, or she's mopping the floors,
     11 or she's wiping the stains from the walls and the doors,
     12 or she's washing the windows, the dishes, the clothes,
     13 or waxing the furniture 'til it just glows,

[1] *scour:* to scrub.
[2] *gleam:* to shine.

14 or cleaning the "fridge,"[3] or the stove or the sink

15 with a lighthearted[4] smile and a friendly wink

16 and she's doing her best to make us think that her soap

(or detergent or cleanser or cleaner or powder or paste or wax or bleach)

17 is the best kind of soap

(or detergent or cleanser or cleaner or powder or paste or wax or bleach)

18 that there is in the whole wide world!

3  19 And maybe it is . . .

20 and maybe it isn't . . .

21 and maybe it does what they say it will do . . .

22 but I'll tell you one thing I know is true:

23 The lady we see when we're watching TV—

24 The lady who smiles as she scours

or scrubs or rubs or washes or wipes or mops or dusts or cleans—

25 or whatever she does on our TV screens—

26 that lady is smiling because she's an actress.

27 And she's earning money for learning those speeches that mention those

wonderful soaps and detergents and cleansers and cleaners and powders and

pastes and waxes and bleaches.

4  28 So the very next time that you happen to be

29 just sitting there quietly watching TV,

30 and you see some nice lady who smiles as she scours or scrubs or rubs or washes

or wipes or mops or dusts or cleans

5  31 remember:

32 Nobody smiles doing housework but those ladies you see on TV.

33 Because even if the soap or detergent or cleanser or cleaner or powder or paste

or wax or bleach—

34 that you use is the very best one—

35 housework is just no fun.

6  36 Children,

37 when you have a house of your own,

38 make sure when there's housework to do that you don't have to do it alone.

39 Little boys, little girls,

40 when you're big husbands and wives,

41 if you want all of the days of your lives to seem sunny as summer weather,

42 make sure when there's housework to do that you do it together.

---

[3] *fridge:* refrigerator.
[4] *lighthearted:* cheerful.

*Source:* Sheldon Harnick, "Housework," from *Free to Be You and Me* (New York: McGraw-Hill, 1974). Reprinted with permission from the Free to Be Foundation, Inc., LLP.

## READING FOR MAIN IDEAS

*Check (✓) the two main ideas in the poem.*

_____ 1. TV commercials (advertisements on TV) give us good information about which soaps and detergents are best.

_____ 2. Men and women should share the housework.

_____ 3. Children shouldn't watch TV because there are too many commercials.

_____ 4. Housework isn't really too much fun.

## READING FOR DETAILS

*Read each sentence. Then look at the stanza mentioned. Find the line or lines in the poem that have the same meaning as the sentence and fill in the line number or numbers.*

1. This person tells us that it's important to buy the right brand of cleaning products.

   *First stanza, line __5__*

2. Usually, women do all of the housework on TV.

   *Second stanza, line _____*

3. She is trying to make us believe that her cleaning product is the best.

   *Second stanza, lines _____, _____, _____*

4. The TV lady's detergent might really be an excellent detergent.

   *Third stanza, lines _____, _____, _____*

5. The lady on TV looks happy because it is her job to look happy.

   *Third stanza, line _____*

6. Only actresses in commercials smile while they do housework. Other people never smile when they do housework.

   *Fifth stanza, line _____*

7. Good cleaning products don't make housework fun.

   *Fifth stanza, lines _____, _____, _____*

**REACTING TO THE READING**

**1** *Read each statement. Check (✓) **Advertisers** if you think the statement is something that the TV advertisers want us to think. Check (✓) **Poet** if you think the statement is something that the poet wants us to think. Discuss your answers with a partner.*

|  | Advertisers | Poet |
|---|:---:|:---:|
| 1. Housework is fun if you have the best detergent. | ❏ | ❏ |
| 2. Housework is never fun. | ❏ | ❏ |
| 3. Most women like doing housework. | ❏ | ❏ |
| 4. Some soaps and detergents are better than others. | ❏ | ❏ |
| 5. Men should do housework, too. | ❏ | ❏ |
| 6. Husbands and wives should share housework if they want to be happy. | ❏ | ❏ |
| 7. It's important to do housework. | ❏ | ❏ |
| 8. Housework is women's work. | ❏ | ❏ |
| 9. The ladies on TV are the only people who smile while they do the housework. | ❏ | ❏ |
| 10. The ladies on TV are smiling because they are using wonderful cleaning products. | ❏ | ❏ |

**2** *Look again at the statements in Exercise 1 above. Which ones do you agree with? Write them below. Compare your opinion with that of a partner. Discuss why you chose the statements you did.*

**Your opinion**

_____

_____

_____

_____

_____

_____

_____

_____

## B    READING TWO: *Good-bye to (Some) Housework*

*Read the following article. Then answer the questions on page 109 about the article. Discuss your answers with a partner.*

# Good-bye to (Some) Housework

**By Hannah Lieker**

1    I can remember a certain TV commercial from when I was a child. In this commercial, a happy housewife is polishing her table. The table is so shiny that we can see her smiling reflection in it. She's so happy about her shiny tabletop! Does shiny furniture make people happy nowadays? Does anyone even polish furniture today? I cannot remember the last time that I polished furniture.

2    People have less time for housework these days. They are lucky if they have time to wipe the crumbs off the table and put the breakfast dishes in the sink before they go to their jobs.

3    Because people have less time, many kinds of chores, like polishing furniture, just don't get done anymore. Some people have studied changes in the use of cleaning products. From their studies, we can tell which chores aren't getting done. For example, one study looked at differences in the types of housework people did between 1986 and 1996. In just ten years, there were many changes.

4    Some chores, like laundry, will never go away. In 1996, people used about the same amount of laundry detergent that they used in 1986. But polishing furniture seems to be less important than doing laundry. In 1986, 21 percent of homemakers[1] used three or more cans of furniture polish in six months. By 1996, only 12 percent of homemakers used that much furniture polish. Carpet cleaning is another endangered chore. In 1986, 9 percent of homemakers used three or more containers of carpet cleaner in six months. By 1996, only 5 percent of homemakers used that much carpet cleaner. And what about those ovens? Seventy-five percent of homemakers used no oven cleaner for six months in 1996!

---

[1] *homemaker:* person in family who is in charge of housework.

*Source:* Statistics from Mediamark Research, Inc. of New York, cited in *American Demographics*, January, 1997.

1. Why are people doing less housework now?

2. Which chore(s) are people doing less often now?

3. Which chore(s) do people do as often today?

## C   LINKING READINGS ONE AND TWO

*The poem in Reading One was written in 1974. The types of housework it mentions may not be done in the same way today. List these chores in the chart under "Yesterday's Chores."*

*Use information from Reading Two to answer the question under "Today's Chores." Sometimes the answer will not be clear from the reading, so you will need to make your best guess. Write* **as much as before** *or* **less than before.**

| Yesterday's Chores (from Reading One) | Today's Chores Do people do this chore *as much as before* or *less than before?* |
| --- | --- |
| Scouring skillets | Less than before |
| | |
| | |
| | |
| | |
| | |
| | |
| | |

*Now discuss the following questions with a partner.*

1. Why did you give the answers you did to the question on the right?

2. Compare yesterday's and today's chores. How are they different?

3. Do you think that people will continue to do less and less housework in the future? Why or why not? Which other chores do you think might disappear?

# 3 Focus on Vocabulary

**1** *Read each group of sentences. Pay attention to the underlined words. Cross out the sentence that does not make sense.*

1. **a.** I <u>happened to</u> be at the supermarket yesterday when they were giving away free boxes of a new detergent!
   **b.** Excuse me, do you <u>happen to</u> have change for a dollar?
   **c.** ~~OK, I'll meet you for lunch tomorrow. I will happen to be there at 12:15.~~

2. **a.** I have a <u>terribly urgent</u> message for Tom. Can you make sure that he gets it this month?
   **b.** This letter is <u>terribly urgent</u>. I think I should send it express mail, so it gets there tomorrow.
   **c.** I'd like to talk to Dr. Donlon, but it's not <u>terribly urgent</u>. She can call me back when she has time.

3. **a.** This detergent doesn't make my clothes really clean. Perhaps I should try a different <u>brand</u>.
   **b.** Bleach is the best <u>brand</u> to use for washing white clothes.
   **c.** Can you buy some detergent for me? Just get the cheapest <u>brand</u>.

4. **a.** The doctor <u>winked</u> when she told the couple their son had a broken leg.
   **b.** My grandpa used to <u>wink</u> when he told a joke.
   **c.** Jim <u>winked</u> at the little girl as he said good-bye to her.

5. **a.** Before the Britney Spears concert, a man came on stage and <u>mentioned</u>, "Here's Britney!"
   **b.** Did you <u>mention</u> the party to Joe? I haven't invited him yet.
   **c.** Please don't <u>mention</u> anything about my vacation plans to my boss. She doesn't think anyone should take vacations.

6. **a.** Diana was surprised when the dinner guests <u>appeared</u> an hour early.
   **b.** My keys have <u>appeared</u>. I can't find them.
   **c.** Every time I cook fish for dinner, Tuca, the neighbor's cat, <u>appears</u> at my back door.

7. **a.** I have a <u>speech</u> with my mom on the telephone every Sunday.
   **b.** The president gave a <u>speech</u> last night about taxes and education.
   **c.** I always get nervous when I have to make <u>speeches</u> in my English class.

8. **a.** Karen wants to be an <u>actress</u>, so she has moved to Hollywood.
   **b.** A new movie with my favorite <u>actress</u> is opening tonight at the Lumiere theater. Do you want to go?
   **c.** You need to be really good at math and geometry if you want to be an actor or an <u>actress</u>.

**2** *Complete the sentences with words from the boxes. Use a word from Box A for the first blank in each item. Use a word from Box B for the second blank.*

| A | | B | |
|---|---|---|---|
| actress | mention | bleach | mop |
| detergent | polish | cleanser | terribly urgent |
| happen to | shine | dust | winked |

1. I don't have time to _____*polish*_____ the furniture, so I am just going to _____*dust*_____ it.

2. _____ makes clothes clean, but _____ makes them white.

3. Can you get some dish soap the next time you _____ be at the store? It's not _____, so don't make a special trip.

4. If you want your floors to _____, use new, improved Twinkle-Floor next time you _____!

5. The woman in the commercial didn't _____ the price of the _____ that she was using to clean the tub.

6. The _____
   accepted her award and said,
   "I couldn't have done it
   without my husband and
   my daughters," as she
   _____ at
   them in the audience.

**3** *Catherine is going on a business trip this week. Her mother arrives on Sunday, immediately after Catherine returns. Catherine's roommate, Jess, said that she will do the housework while Catherine is away. Complete the note that Catherine leaves for Jess.*

---

Jess—

Thanks for doing the housework this weekend while I am in Atlanta. It will be nice to have a clean apartment when my mother arrives on Sunday morning. Here are some of the most important chores.

Please <u>mop the kitchen floor and clean the refrigerator</u>_____.

Also, _____.

And if you have time, please _____

_____.

I have bought some _____ for you to use when

you _____.

*(add your own sentences here)*

_____

_____

_____

_____

_____

_____

_____.


Thanks again!

See you Saturday night.

Catherine

---

# 4 Focus on Writing

## A STYLE: Poetry

**1** *Read the first stanza of the poem in Reading One out loud several times to yourself. Then read the first paragraph of the text in Reading Two out loud several times. Why does the poem sound different?*

### Writing Rhymes

Poems often use words that rhyme with each other. Usually, the words that rhyme are at the end of different lines, but sometimes they are in the same line. Two words rhyme if their endings sound the same.

*There is a young girl named (Tess,)*

*Who's always a terrible (mess.)*

*She starts each day (clean,)*

*But by eight-(fifteen,)*

*Breakfast's all over her (dress.)*

**2** *Look at the first stanza of "Housework." Find the words that rhyme. Circle the words, and connect them with lines.*

"You know, there are times when we happen to (be),

just sitting there quietly watching (TV),

when the program we're watching will stop for awhile,

and suddenly someone appears with a smile,

and starts to show us how terribly urgent

it is to buy some brand of detergent

or soap or cleanser or cleaner or powder or paste or wax or bleach—

to help with the housework."

**3** *Put the words in the box into lists of words that rhyme. Then add some more words that you know to each list. One word has been done for you.*

| | | | | |
|---|---|---|---|---|
| awhile | doors | jeans | must | pop |
| beans | drop | means | none | run |
| ~~chores~~ | hop | mile | pile | trust |
| done | | | | |

| Floors | Cleans | Fun | Smile | Mop | Dust |
|--------|--------|-----|-------|-----|------|
| *chores* | _____ | _____ | _____ | _____ | _____ |
| _____ | _____ | _____ | _____ | _____ | _____ |
| _____ | _____ | _____ | _____ | _____ | _____ |
| _____ | _____ | _____ | _____ | _____ | _____ |
| _____ | _____ | _____ | _____ | _____ | _____ |

**4** *Work in pairs. Write two sets of two lines about housework, and end the lines with words that rhyme. Use some of the words in Exercise 3.*

**Examples:**  I don't like mopping floors.

It's the worst of all the chores!

I never clean my sinks.

That's why my house stinks!

1. _____

_____

2. _____

_____

*Now share your "poems" with the class.*

## B  GRAMMAR:  Adverbs and Expressions of Frequency

**1** *Read the following e-mail, and underline the words and phrases that tell how often someone does something.*

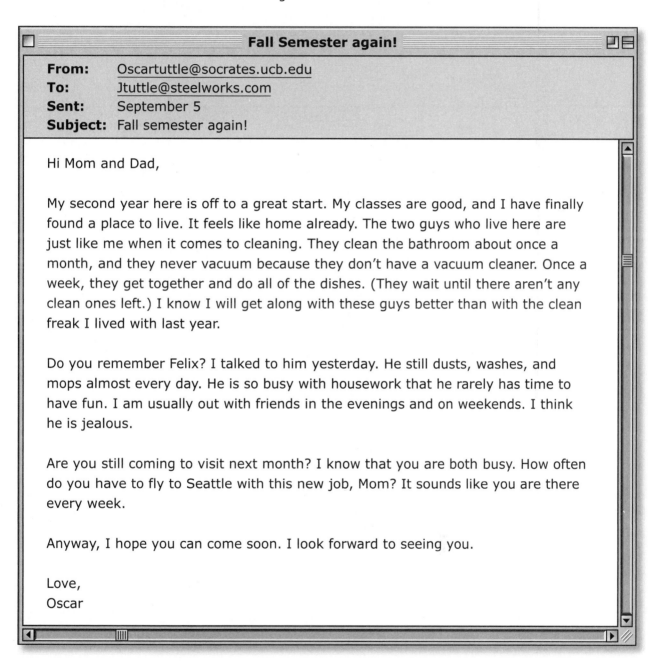

**Fall Semester again!**

| | |
|---|---|
| **From:** | Oscartuttle@socrates.ucb.edu |
| **To:** | Jtuttle@steelworks.com |
| **Sent:** | September 5 |
| **Subject:** | Fall semester again! |

Hi Mom and Dad,

My second year here is off to a great start. My classes are good, and I have finally found a place to live. It feels like home already. The two guys who live here are just like me when it comes to cleaning. They clean the bathroom about once a month, and they never vacuum because they don't have a vacuum cleaner. Once a week, they get together and do all of the dishes. (They wait until there aren't any clean ones left.) I know I will get along with these guys better than with the clean freak I lived with last year.

Do you remember Felix? I talked to him yesterday. He still dusts, washes, and mops almost every day. He is so busy with housework that he rarely has time to have fun. I am usually out with friends in the evenings and on weekends. I think he is jealous.

Are you still coming to visit next month? I know that you are both busy. How often do you have to fly to Seattle with this new job, Mom? It sounds like you are there every week.

Anyway, I hope you can come soon. I look forward to seeing you.

Love,
Oscar

*Now answer the following questions.*

1. What are the words and phrases you underlined?

2. Which verb tense does the writer use in sentences with these words and phrases?

## Adverbs and Expressions of Frequency

1. Adverbs and expressions of frequency describe **how often** someone does something.

   They **never** vacuum because they don't have a vacuum cleaner.
   **Once a week,** they do all the dishes.

2. The verbs used with adverbs and expressions of frequency are usually in the **simple present tense.**

   He **rarely** *has* time to have fun.
   He *mops* the floors **every day.**

3. Adverbs of frequency (*always, usually, often, sometimes, rarely, never*) usually go after the verb **be.**

   I *am usually* out with friends in the evenings and on weekends.

   But they usually go before other verbs.

   I **rarely** *stay* at home.

4. **Expressions of frequency** (like *every day, once a week,* or *twice a month*) usually go at the beginning or at the end of a sentence.

   **Once a month,** they clean the bathroom.
   They clean the bathroom **once a month.**

5. Use *How often . . . ?* in **questions** about frequency.

   **How often** do you have to fly to Seattle?

**2** *Felix is looking for another roommate. He went to a roommate agency and filled out a questionnaire. Read the first part of the questionnaire.*

## ROOMMATES FOR YOU

To help us find you the best roommate, please answer the following questions:

Name: ___Felix M. Jefferson, Jr.___

### Describe yourself

| How often . . . | Never | Rarely | Sometimes | Usually | Always |
|---|---|---|---|---|---|
| . . . do you smoke in the house? | ✓ | | | | |
| . . . do you watch TV in the evenings? | | ✓ | | | |
| . . . do you have dinner guests? | ✓ | | | | |
| . . . do you listen to the radio or CDs? | | ✓ | | | |
| . . . are you at home on the weekends? | | | | ✓ | |
| . . . do you go to sleep before 11 P.M.? | | | | | ✓ |

*Now read the second part of the questionnaire.*

---

**Housekeeping**

Answer the following questions with the frequency of each activity

(e.g., 1X/week = once a week, 2X/month = twice a month).

How often do you . . .

. . . vacuum the carpets?    __2X/week__

. . . dust the furniture?    __1X/week__

. . . mop the floors?    __every day__

. . . clean the bathroom?    __3X/week__

. . . wash the windows?    __every week__

. . . clean the oven?    __2X/month__

---

*Rewrite the following sentences to tell how often Felix does these things. Use the information in the questionnaire.*

1. Felix smokes in the house.

   _Felix never smokes in the house._ _____

2. He listens to the radio or CDs.

   _____

3. He has dinner guests.

   _____

4. He is in bed by 11 P.M.

   _____

5. He vacuums the carpets.

   _____

6. He cleans the bathroom.

   _____

7. He washes the windows.

   _____

**3** *Write questions with **How often ... you ...** about the following chores. Then ask a partner these questions and write your partner's answers.*

1. mop the floors

    A: How often *do you mop the floor?* _____

    B: _____

2. wash the dishes

    A: How often _____

    B: _____

3. clean the bathroom

    A: How often _____

    B: _____

4. dust the furniture

    A: How often _____

    B: _____

5. stay up late

    A: How often _____

    B: _____

6. invite people to your home

    A: How often _____

    B: _____

7. do laundry

    A: How often _____

    B: _____

**4** *Look at your partner's answers in Exercise 3 above. Who do you think your partner would prefer to live with, Oscar or Felix? Write a short paragraph giving your reasons for your opinion.*

I think _____ would prefer to live with _____

because _____

_____

_____

## C  WRITING TOPICS

*Choose one of the following topics. Write one paragraph. Use some of the vocabulary, grammar, and style that you learned in this unit.*

1. Write a poem about housework. Use some rhyming words.

2. Who does the housework in your house? Write about different chores. Who usually does these chores? Who sometimes does them? Who never does them? Does everyone share in the housework? Do some people do more housework than other people?

3. Find a magazine ad or a TV commercial for a cleaning product. Does it have a smiling woman, like the one in the poem? Describe the person in this ad or commercial. What is the person doing? Does the person look happy?

4. Find an ad or commercial for a cleaning product. Describe it. According to this ad or commercial, why should people buy the product? Who do you think the advertisers are trying to sell the product to—women who work outside the home, women who stay at home, all women, both women and men?

## D  RESEARCH TOPIC

*What do people in your community think about housework? To answer this question, you need to take a survey. Follow these steps:*

1. Work in a small group. Write five questions, and make a questionnaire. (See the example on page 120.) You will need to make copies to give to the people that you survey.

2. In your group, decide where each person will hand out the questionnaire. One person might go to a shopping center, and one person might go to a bus stop, for example.

   You also need to decide who you will survey. For example, how many men and how many women will you survey? Do you want to survey people of different ages? Do you want to survey people who live alone and people who have families?

3. Each person should survey at least five people. Tell people what you are doing when you approach them. You might say, "Hi, My name is _____. I am doing some research about housework for a class I'm taking. Do you have a couple of minutes to fill out my questionnaire?" Be sure to thank people for their time.

4. When you have all of your answers, you need to count the answers for each question.

5. Write up the results of your survey and report back to the class. Listen to the other surveys. Is your community full of Oscars or full of Felixes?

# SAMPLE QUESTIONNAIRE

Please take a few minutes to answer the following questions! Thank you very much!

**Sex:**   M◯   F◯

**Age:**   20–30 ◯   30–50 ◯   50–70 ◯

**Single:** ◯   **Married:** ◯

**Comments**

1. Do you clean your oven at least once a year?   YES◯   NO◯   _____

2. Do you do laundry at least twice a month?   YES◯   NO◯   _____

3. Do you vacuum at least once a week?   YES◯   NO◯   _____

4. Do you ever polish the furniture in your home?   YES◯   NO◯   _____

5. Do you do as much housework as your parents did?   YES◯   NO◯   _____

For step-by-step practice in the writing process, see the *Writing Activity Book, Basic/Low Intermediate, Second Edition,* Unit 6.

| | |
|---|---|
| Assignment: | Writing an Opinion Paragraph |
| Prewriting: | Freewriting |
| Organizing: | Supporting an Opinion |
| Revising: | Writing Concluding Sentences |
| | Using Adverbs of Frequency |
| Editing: | Correcting Sentence Fragments |

For Unit 6 Internet activities, visit the NorthStar Companion Website at http://www.longman.com/northstar.

# Organic Produce: Is It Worth the Price?

# 1 Focus on the Topic

## A PREDICTING

Look at the picture, and discuss these questions with the class.

1. Where do you buy fruits and vegetables?

2. How do you choose the fruits and vegetables you buy? What do you look for?

3. Read the title of the unit. What do you think it means?

# B   SHARING INFORMATION

*When you shop, how do you choose your fruit? Do you choose it by its color? Do you choose it by its size? For each kind of fruit, check (✓) each box that shows how you choose that fruit. Add a fruit of your choice to the list.*

| Fruit | Color | Size | Softness/ Hardness | Smell | Price |
|---|---|---|---|---|---|
| Apples | ❑ | ❑ | ❑ | ❑ | ❑ |
| Bananas | ❑ | ❑ | ❑ | ❑ | ❑ |
| Oranges | ❑ | ❑ | ❑ | ❑ | ❑ |
| Pears | ❑ | ❑ | ❑ | ❑ | ❑ |
| Melons | ❑ | ❑ | ❑ | ❑ | ❑ |
| Strawberries | ❑ | ❑ | ❑ | ❑ | ❑ |
| _____ | ❑ | ❑ | ❑ | ❑ | ❑ |

*In a small group, share and discuss your answers. For example, if you checked "size" for apples, what size do you look for? Why?*

# C   PREPARING TO READ

## BACKGROUND

*Look at the picture on page 123 of a produce section of a grocery store. There are many kinds of fruits and vegetables. A few are organic (see the signs). The others are not—they are regular fruits and vegetables. Use the information in the picture to complete these sentences.*

1. Regular apples cost  *$1.39 a pound*_____.

2. Organic apples cost _____.

3. Regular pears cost _____.

4. Organic pears cost _____.

5. Red leaf lettuce costs _____.

6. Green leaf lettuce costs _____.

7. Organic green leaf lettuce costs _____.

8. _____ lettuce is the most expensive lettuce.

*Why do you think organic fruits and vegetables are more expensive than regular fruits and vegetables? Discuss this question with your classmates.*

## VOCABULARY FOR COMPREHENSION

**1** *Read the sentences. Try to understand the underlined words without looking them up in a dictionary.*

1. Orange juice really is orange. But many sodas are made with <u>artificial</u> colors. These colors come from chemicals.

2. Sometimes bananas are green and hard. To <u>ripen</u> them, put them in a paper bag. In one or two days, they should be yellow and soft.

3. Some fruits, like apples, grow on trees. Some, like blackberries, grow on bushes. And some, like grapes, grow on <u>vines</u>.

4. Growing your own tomatoes is difficult, but <u>it's worth</u> the work. Tomatoes from your own garden are better than tomatoes from the store.

5. The <u>old-fashioned</u> way to make ice cream took a lot of time and hard work. Today, the way we make ice cream is fast and easy.

6. <u>Fresh</u> fruit tastes much better than fruit from a can.

*Now match the words with their definitions.*

__e__  1. artificial                    **a.** become ready to eat

_____  2. ripen                         **b.** not modern or new

_____  3. vine                          **c.** it will be useful, you will gain from it

_____  4. it's worth it                 **d.** not canned or frozen

_____  5. old-fashioned                 **e.** not natural

_____  6. fresh                         **f.** a plant that grows up and around a stick

**2** *Read the sentences. Try to understand the underlined words without looking them up in a dictionary. Then use the underlined words to complete the chart. Some words are the names of the categories. Other words are examples of things that belong in the categories.*

1. You'll find bananas in the <u>produce</u> section of your supermarket or grocery store.

2. I hate <u>insects</u>! Mosquitoes bite me every time I go outside, and ants get into all the food in my cupboards.

3. Sometimes I have trouble growing vegetables, but I never have trouble growing <u>weeds</u>! They just take over the garden.

4. Farmers use <u>pesticides</u> and <u>herbicides</u> to kill insects and weeds.

5. <u>Cancer</u> kills millions of people every year.

6. These tomatoes don't look very nice, but they <u>taste</u> wonderful.

| Chemicals | _____ | Plants | Senses | _____ | Illnesses |
|---|---|---|---|---|---|
| 1. _____ | 1. apples | 1. flowers | 1. feel | 1. mosquitoes | 1. the flu |
| 2. _____ | 2. oranges | 2. vegetables | 2. smell | 2. flies | 2. a cold |
| | 3. broccoli | 3. trees | 3. hear | 3. ants | 3. AIDS |
| | 4. lettuce | 4. _____ | 4. see | | 4. _____ |
| | | | 5. _____ | | |

# 2 Focus on Reading

*Mr. Green has a newspaper advice column called "Ask Mr. Green."  People with shopping problems write to him.  Read this letter to Mr. Green.  The writer asks two questions.  How will Mr. Green answer these questions?  Write your ideas for each answer on the lines that follow.*

> **Dear Mr. Green:**
>
> Lately I see more and more "organic" fruits and vegetables in the supermarkets. I'm confused. Often the organic apples or strawberries aren't as red or as large as the regular ones. They sometimes have spots or insect holes. Also, organic produce can cost three times as much as regular produce! So, tell me, what exactly are organic fruits and vegetables? And why are they so expensive?
>
> *Confused Shopper*
> *Bakersfield, CA*

1. _____

   _____

2. _____

   _____

*Organic fruits (left) vs. regular fruits (right)*

*Now read Mr. Green's answer. Were your ideas correct?*

# ASK MR. GREEN:
# Organic Produce vs. Regular Produce

**Dear Confused Shopper:**

1   You're right. Sometimes organic produce doesn't look as nice as regular produce, and it generally costs up to 50 percent more. Let me explain why.

2   Since about 1950, farmers in the United States have used chemicals to grow their fruits and vegetables. They use pesticides to kill insects that eat their plants. They use herbicides to kill the weeds that kill their plants. These chemicals are a great help to farmers. By using them, farmers can grow more produce on the same amount of land. This means that shoppers can find more produce in the stores.

3   Farmers even use chemicals to artificially ripen fruits and vegetables. Most tomatoes, for example, are picked from the vine while they are still green. They are put in a box to go to a supermarket. They turn red (ripen) because of a chemical put in the box with the tomatoes. Because produce can be picked early, it can travel long distances to stores. As a result, we can find most kinds of fruits and vegetables all year long.

4   Some people argue, however, that there are problems with using all these chemicals. When we eat produce, we're also eating a little bit of the chemicals. Over time, these chemicals build up in our bodies. Some scientists believe that this buildup of chemicals can even cause cancer. Because of worries like these, some farmers now grow produce the old-fashioned way—without chemicals. We call this kind of produce *organic*.

5   Organic produce is more expensive than other produce for several reasons. Many organic farmers can't grow as much produce as other farmers. Their farms tend to be smaller, and, of course, they don't use herbicides and pesticides. Also, because no chemicals are used, the produce has to arrive at the store very soon after it's picked. This too, costs money.

6   Is organic produce worth the extra cost? Should you buy organic produce or regular produce? That's up to you. But if you're not familiar with organic produce, you might want to try it. More and more shoppers are buying organic produce. Many of these shoppers say that they're not just concerned about their health. They say organic fruits and vegetables taste fresher and better.

*Mr. Green*

## READING FOR MAIN IDEAS

*Check (✓) the ideas that Mr. Green discussed in his letter.*

\_\_\_\_\_ **1.** He explained how much organic fruits and vegetables cost.

\_\_\_\_\_ **2.** He discussed the first farmers to grow organic produce.

\_\_\_\_\_ **3.** He discussed the use of chemicals in growing regular produce.

\_\_\_\_\_ **4.** He explained why regular produce may be bad for your health.

\_\_\_\_\_ **5.** He explained what organic produce is.

\_\_\_\_\_ **6.** He explained why organic fruits and vegetables are expensive.

\_\_\_\_\_ **7.** He explained where people can buy organic produce.

## READING FOR DETAILS

*Read each statement. Decide if it is true or false. Write **T** (true) or **F** (false) next to it. If the statement is false, write a true statement after it.*

_F_ **1.** Organic produce looks the same as regular produce.

*Organic produce doesn't look as nice as regular produce.*

\_\_\_\_\_ **2.** Organic produce generally costs up to 50 percent more than regular produce.

_____

\_\_\_\_\_ **3.** Herbicides kill insects.

_____

\_\_\_\_\_ **4.** Some scientists believe that chemical buildup can cause heart problems.

_____

\_\_\_\_\_ **5.** Organic fruits and vegetables are ripened with chemicals.

_____

\_\_\_\_\_ **6.** With chemicals, farmers can grow more produce on the same amount of land.

_____

\_\_\_\_\_ **7.** Organic produce has to arrive at stores quickly.

_____

## REACTING TO THE READING

**1** *Read each statement. Would Mr. Green agree or disagree with that statement? Check (✓)* **Agree** *or* **Disagree.** *Use the information in his letter to decide.*

|  | Agree | Disagree |
|---|---|---|
| 1. Organic produce tastes better. | ❑ | ❑ |
| 2. Tomatoes should be picked from the vine while they are still green. | ❑ | ❑ |
| 3. The only way to kill weeds and insects is to use chemicals. | ❑ | ❑ |
| 4. It's worth the extra cost to buy organic produce. | ❑ | ❑ |
| 5. If the farmers didn't use chemicals, grocery stores wouldn't have as many vegetables to sell. | ❑ | ❑ |
| 6. Organic farmers make a lot of money because the produce is so expensive. | ❑ | ❑ |

**2** *Read each quote. Decide whether the person who said it would probably buy organic or regular produce. Write* **organic** *or* **regular** *next to the quote. Then discuss your answers with a partner.*

_____organic_____ 1. "I think that nowadays even the air we breathe is harmful."

_____ 2. "I don't want to wait until summer for strawberries."

_____ 3. "I like apples that taste like the apples we picked off trees when I was a kid."

_____ 4. "I'm trying not to spend much money on food this month."

_____ 5. "It might sound silly, but I always want the things that look the nicest."

_____ 6. "I don't want to feed my children any food that might not be healthy for them."

**3** *What about you? Do you buy organic or regular produce? Why? Discuss with a partner. Give your opinions. Write them down below.*

**Your opinion**

_____

_____

_____

_____

**Your partner's opinion**

_____

_____

_____

_____

## B    READING TWO: *What's in Our Food?*

Chemicals aren't just used to grow produce. They are also used to keep foods fresh, give them color, or change the taste. *Natural food*, including organic food, is food that doesn't have any chemicals or other artificial ingredients.

*Look quickly at the two soup can labels below. Answer the questions.*

    **a.** Which soup is natural? _____

    **b.** Which soup has artificial ingredients? _____

*Now read the labels more carefully. Then work in a small group to answer the questions on page 130.*

### WHAT'S IN OUR FOOD?

Label 1: Gordon's Soup         Label 2: Health Country Soup

| **Nutrition Facts** | | |
|---|---|---|
| Serving[1] Size ½ cup (120 ml) | | |
| Servings per Container 2.5 | | |
| **Amount Per Serving** | | |
| **Calories** 80  Calories from Fat 20 | | |
| | | **% Daily Value[2]** |
| **Total Fat** 2g | | 3% |
| Saturated Fat 1g | | 5% |
| **Cholesterol** 10mg | | 3% |
| **Sodium** 810mg | | 34% |
| **Total Carbohydrate** 10g | | 3% |
| Dietary Fiber 2g | | 8% |
| Sugars 2g | | |
| **Protein** 5g | | |
| Vitamin A 40% | Vitamin C 0% | |
| Calcium 2% | Iron 4% | |

**Ingredients:** potatoes, carrots, water, green beans, peas, salt, onions, celery, tomato paste, vegetable oil, monosodium glutamate, caramel color, sugar.

| **Nutrition Facts** | | |
|---|---|---|
| Serving[1] Size 1 cup (240 g) | | |
| Servings per Container 2 | | |
| **Amount Per Serving** | | |
| **Calories** 80  Calories from Fat 0 | | |
| | | **% Daily Value[2]** |
| **Total Fat** 0g | | 0% |
| Saturated Fat 0g | | 0% |
| **Cholesterol** 0mg | | 0% |
| **Sodium** 250mg | | 10% |
| **Total Carbohydrate** 17g | | 6% |
| Dietary Fiber 4g | | 16% |
| Sugars 8g | | |
| **Protein** 6g | | |
| Vitamin A 200% | Vitamin C 25% | |
| Calcium 4% | Iron 10% | |

**Ingredients:** water, organic carrots, organic tomatoes, organic celery, organic potatoes, organic peas, organic green beans, tomato paste, small white beans, honey, organic lima beans, organic onions, organic broccoli, organic cabbage, organic cauliflower, organic spinach, sea salt, organic green peppers, garlic, lemon juice, pepper, parsley, nutmeg, bay leaves, sage, basil, oregano.

---

[1] *serving:* an amount for one person.
[2] *% daily value:* how much the food gives you of what a person needs in a day.

1. Which can has more soup? _____

2. Which soup has more fat per serving? _____

3. Which soup has more sodium (salt) per serving? _____

4. Which soup has more protein per serving? _____

5. Which soup has more vitamins and minerals (calcium, iron) per serving?

_____

6. Which vegetables are in both soups? _____

_____

7. What vegetables, if any, are in the Health Country Soup but not in the

Gordon's Soup? _____

_____

8. What vegetables, if any, are in the Gordon's Soup but not in the Health

Country Soup? _____

9. What difference is there between the vegetables in the Gordon's Soup and

the vegetables in the Health Country Soup? _____

_____

10. Spices are natural ingredients added to foods to make them taste better and

more interesting. What spices do you recognize on these labels? Which soup

has these spices? _____

_____

11. What other ingredients do you see on the Gordon's Soup label? Why do you

think these ingredients are added to the soup? _____

_____

12. Which soup do you think is better for you? _____

Discuss why.

## C    LINKING READINGS ONE AND TWO

You are the chef at a small restaurant. Many customers are asking for soup, so you want to add a homemade vegetable soup to your menu. You have two vegetable soup recipes. One is a soup like Health Country Soup—it uses lots of organic vegetables. The other soup is like Gordon's Soup—it uses regular vegetables, and few of them. Which recipe should you use?

*Work in a small group. Think about and discuss the following things. Then make your decision.*

- **Taste:** Which soup will customers like better?

- **Time:** How long will these soups take to make?

- **Availability of produce:** Will you be able to find the vegetables you need all year long?

- **Price:** Which soup will cost less for you (and your customers), the organic soup or the other soup?

Your decision: _____

*Discuss your decision and the reasons for it with the class.*

# 3 Focus on Vocabulary

**1** *Cross out the word or phrase that is not related to the boldfaced word.*

1. **herbicides:** ~~insects~~, weeds, farms

2. **ripe:** yellow banana, green strawberry, red apple

3. **vines:** tomatoes, grapes, apples

4. **natural:** stone, wood, plastic

5. **artificial:** caramel color, monosodium glutamate, carrot

6. **produce:** potato, apple, soup

7. **it's worth it:** it will be a problem, it will be useful, you'll gain by it

8. **taste:** bad, hard, fresh

9. **old-fashioned:** milking cows by hand, separating eggs with an electric machine, planting corn with a stick

10. **fresh:** tomatoes from the can, grapes off the vine, apples from the tree

11. **insect:** bee, bird, fly

**2** *Read the conversation between a radio program interviewer and a farmer. Complete the conversation, using the words in the box.*

| | | | |
|---|---|---|---|
| fresh | it's worth it | pesticides | tastes |
| herbicides | natural | produce | vines |
| insects | old-fashioned | ripen | weeds |

INTERVIEWER:    Today I'm talking to Mr. Robinson, who runs an organic farm in Iowa. We're in a field with many (**1**) _____vines_____ full of tomatoes that are starting to (**2**) _____. Mr. Robinson, can you tell us about organic farming?

MR. ROBINSON:    Well, organic farming is the (**3**) _____ way of farming. I grow (**4**) _____ without using (**5**) _____ to kill weeds or (**6**) _____ to kill insects.

INTERVIEWER:    How do you keep (**7**) _____ from eating your plants?

MR. ROBINSON:    Well, I do lose some plants to them. But there are many things I can do. For example . . . Do you see the little yellow flowers next to the tomatoes? They are marigolds. The insects don't like the smell of the marigolds, so they stay away from the tomatoes. This method is easy and it's (**8**) _____.

INTERVIEWER:    What else do you do?

MR. ROBINSON:    I make sure I get rid of all the (**9**) _____ because they're plants I don't want, and harmful insects like them. And then, believe it or not, some insects are good insects. They don't harm plants, and they kill insects that do harm plants. So I make sure there are lots of good insects here.

INTERVIEWER:    All this sounds like a lot of work.

MR. ROBINSON:    It is hard work, but (**10**) _____. People want produce that (**11**) _____ (**12**) _____. I grow it for them!

**3** *Look back at Exercise 2C, on page 131. Which soup recipe did you decide to use for your restaurant? Imagine that as the chef of this restaurant you need to write a memo to your manager explaining why you chose this soup. In the space provided, write at least four sentences. Use the categories from 2C to help you. Be sure to use at least one word from the box in each sentence.*

| | | | | |
|---|---|---|---|---|
| artificial | it's worth it | old-fashioned | produce | taste |
| fresh | natural | organic | ripe | vines |
| herbicides | non-organic | pesticides | ripen | |

### Chez Arthur

TO:     Manager

FROM: Chef

DATE:  12/11


I've decided to make the _____ soup for the winter menu.

I made this decision after careful consideration of the following:


**Taste:** _____

_____

**Time:** _____

_____

**Availability of produce:** _____

_____

**Price:** _____

_____


Let me know if you agree with my decision.

# 4 Focus on Writing

## A STYLE: Audience

**1** *Look again at the letters from Confused Shopper and Mr. Green on pages 125 and 126. Then discuss these questions with a partner.*

1. Why did Confused Shopper and Mr. Green write these letters?

2. How do these letters seem different from letters that you would write to a friend?

*Now read the answers to these questions.*

Confused Shopper wrote to Mr. Green for one specific reason: to get answers to questions about organic produce. Mr. Green wrote to give Confused Shopper those answers. So their letters are very different from letters you would write to a friend.

When Mr. Green wrote to Confused Shopper, he was also writing to the people who read the newspaper where his advice column "Ask Mr. Green" appears. Confused Shopper and the newspaper readers are the audience for Mr. Green's letters.

### Audience, Content, and Tone

In any kind of writing, **audience** refers to the people who read what you write. What you say—**content**—and how you say it—**tone**—will depend on your audience.

#### Tips on content

- Write about what your audience needs to know.

- Write about what will interest your audience.

- Write about what will be appropriate for your audience. A letter to a friend will probably be about everyday, personal things. A letter to a boss will probably be about professional things only.

#### Tips on tone

- A letter to a close friend may have a lot of slang and may sound very casual. A letter to a teacher or a boss will not use any slang and will be more formal.

- When you write to a friend, you can express negative emotions like anger. When you write to a teacher, to a boss, or to people you don't know, you should avoid expressing these emotions directly.

**2** *Read the following note. Then read the statements below. Circle the correct word(s) to complete these statements about audience, content, and tone.*

---

Hi Matt,

   I won't be home until 7:30. Can you go to the store? I want to make spaghetti and a salad for dinner, but we don't have everything we need. And we also need some food for the weekend.

   For tonight, can you get some spaghetti, some onions, some lettuce, and tomatoes? And how about a watermelon for dessert?

   We'll need bread and eggs for breakfast tomorrow. I noticed that we're almost out of rice and milk. I also thought it would be nice to have some more fruit in the house. Could you buy bananas and grapes? Oh, and how about a cake for dessert, too?

   If you go to Rainbow Grocery, buy all organic produce.

See you later.

Love,

Alice

---

**1.** Matt is Alice's boss / husband / young son.

**2.** The content is about work / everyday household items / personal topics.

**3.** The tone is formal / informal.

**3** *Mr. Green wrote magazine articles about organic food for three different magazines. Read the information about the three magazines.*

- *Mother's World* is a magazine for mothers. It gives advice on food, schools, and many other topics.

- *Garden Times* is for people who have homes with gardens, and who like to grow flowers and perhaps some fruits and vegetables for their families.

- *Farming News* is for professional farmers; it gives them the latest information about farming.

*The following sentences come from the three magazine articles that Mr. Green wrote. Read each group of sentences and decide which magazine they come from. Discuss your answers with a partner.*

1. Growing organic vegetables is not as hard as you think. In fact, it might be easier and more fun. Instead of using chemicals to keep out insects, try planting flowers that keep insects away from your vegetables.

   _____ magazine

2. Ten years ago, few people were willing to pay the higher prices for organic produce. But today you'll find that many people will spend more money to buy fruits and vegetables that are free of pesticides and herbicides.

   _____ magazine

3. Eating organic fruits and vegetables is one way to better health. Organic produce is healthy because it is grown naturally without any chemicals.

   _____ magazine

**4** *The following sentences come from two different letters. One, addressed to the manager of a school cafeteria, tells why the cafeteria should serve organic produce. The other letter, addressed to a friend who always eats organic food, tells about the cafeteria. Read each sentence and decide which letter it is from. Check (✓) **To Manager** or **To Friend**. Discuss your choices with a partner.*

|  | To Manager | To Friend |
|---|---|---|
| 1. Organic produce is healthier because it is grown without chemicals. | ❑ | ❑ |
| 2. Isn't that crazy—no organic produce! | ❑ | ❑ |
| 3. I am certain that the cafeteria will attract more customers if it decides to serve organic produce. | ❑ | ❑ |
| 4. Thank you for considering my request for organic produce. | ❑ | ❑ |
| 5. Take care. I'll see you soon! | ❑ | ❑ |
| 6. You wouldn't believe the problems I'm having with that bad cafeteria. | ❑ | ❑ |
| 7. I am writing to bring a problem to your attention: The cafeteria does not serve organic produce. | ❑ | ❑ |
| 8. Many people believe that organic produce tastes better than other produce. | ❑ | ❑ |

**5** On a separate piece of paper, write the letter to the cafeteria manager. Use the sentences in Exercise 4 on page 136 and some sentences of your own. Begin the letter with "Dear Sir or Madam," and close it with "Sincerely," and your name. (For more on letter writing, see page 69.)

## B    GRAMMAR: Count and Non-Count Nouns

**1** Read the note on page 135 again. Underline all the food words in the second paragraph. Then answer these questions.

1. Which words are singular? What word comes before a singular word?

2. Which words are plural? What is the last letter in the plural words?

### Count and Non-Count Nouns*

| | Singular | Plural |
|---|---|---|
| **1. Count nouns** refer to people or things that can be counted. They can be singular or plural. | one **shopper** <br> one **vegetable** | two **shoppers** <br> two **vegetables** |
| Use **a** or **an** before a singular count noun. Plural count nouns need only **-s** or **-es** at the end of the word. Numbers can be used with count nouns. | I need **an onion.** <br> I need **a tomato.** <br> I need **one carrot.** | I need **onions.** <br> I need **tomatoes.** <br> I need **two carrots**. |
| **2. Non-count nouns** refer to things that cannot be counted. Do not use *a*, *an*, or a number before non-count nouns. Do not add -s/-es to non-count nouns: they do not have a plural form. | I buy **produce** at the supermarket. <br> We have **bread.** <br> I drink **milk.** | |
| **3. Some** can be used with plural count nouns and non-count nouns in affirmative statements. | I need **some onions.** (*count*) <br> I need **some milk.** (*non-count*) | |
| **4.** Use **any** with plural count nouns and non-count nouns in negative statements. | I don't have **any onions.** (*count*) <br> I don't have **any milk.** (*non-count*) | |
| **5. A lot of** can be used with plural count nouns and with non-count nouns. | I need **a lot of onions.** (*count*) <br> I need **a lot of milk.** (*non-count*) | |

---

* Count nouns and non-count nouns can also be called *countable nouns* and *uncountable nouns*.

**2** *Find all the food items in the note on page 135 and do the following tasks. Then check your answers with classmates.*

**1.** Circle all the singular count nouns.

**2.** Put a square around all the plural count nouns.

**3.** Underline all the non-count nouns two times.

**3** *Complete this paragraph with count nouns and non-count nouns. Make the nouns plural where necessary.*

After reading Alice's note, Matt went to the store. He bought

_____eggs_____, _____, _____,
  1. (egg)              2. (rice)            3. (spaghetti)

_____, and _____. The store didn't have any
  4. (milk)                5. (bread)

organic _____. So, he went to the health food store and bought
           6. (produce)

_____, _____, _____, and
  7. (lettuce)         8. (tomato)          9. (banana)

_____. But he forgot to buy a _____.
  10. (grape)                                11. (watermelon)

**4** *Work with a partner. Read the situation and the recipe below. Then look at what Alice has in her cupboard on page 139.*

Alice wants to make garden burgers. She looks at her recipe and the list of ingredients. She knows she has a lot of milk and eggs in her refrigerator, but she isn't sure about the other ingredients. Does she have them in her cupboard?

| GARDEN BURGERS | | | |
|---|---|---|---|
| **Ingredients** | | | |
| 3 cups of walnuts | 2 cups of rolled oats | 1 teaspoon salt | 1/4 cup of oil (for frying) |
| 1 carrot, 1 onion | 4 eggs | 1/4 teaspoon pepper | 3 cups of water |
| 1 green pepper | 1/2 cup milk | | |
| | | | |
| **Directions** | | | |
| Chop walnuts and vegetables. Mix the chopped walnuts and vegetables with oats, eggs, milk, salt, and pepper. Make small balls, about 3 inches across. Make the balls flat with the back of a spoon and fry in hot oil until brown. Add water to pan and cook patties in boiling water for 25 minutes. | | | |

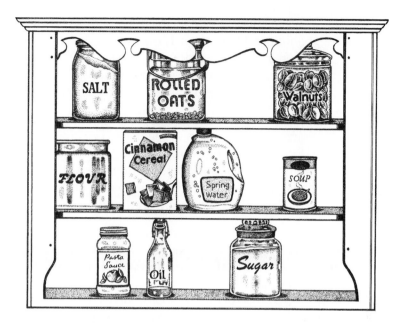

Now write sentences about what Alice has a lot of, what she has but needs to buy more of, and what she doesn't have. Use **a lot of, some,** and **not . . . any.** Use **a** and **an** with singular count nouns.

1. *She has a lot of walnuts. She doesn't need to buy any.*

2. *She has some rolled oats, but she needs to buy more.*

3. *She doesn't have any carrots. She needs to buy some.*

4. _____

5. _____

6. _____

7. _____

8. _____

9. _____

## C  WRITING TOPICS

*Choose one of the following topics. Use some of the vocabulary, grammar, and style that you learned in this unit.*

1. Think of a recipe that you like and know how to cook. Write the recipe. You can use the recipe on page 138 as a model. First list the ingredients. Then write the directions for cooking. (The directions should be in the imperative; that is, use the base form of the verb.) Be sure to pay attention to count nouns and non-count nouns.

2. Write a letter to Mr. Green. (You might want to read the letter by Confused Shopper again, page 125.) In your letter, first tell about something you have seen in stores and don't understand. Then ask one or two questions about it. For example, maybe you have seen tomatoes that say "vine-ripened." But you thought all tomatoes grew on vines. So what does "vine-ripened" mean?

3. Write a short explanation (one or two paragraphs) of organic food for an article in a children's magazine. The children who read the magazine are 8 to 12 years old. Most of them live in big cities, and most are not familiar with organic food. Before you write the explanation, think of your audience and of the content and tone that would be best. What will interest your readers? What will they need to know?

## D RESEARCH TOPIC

*Work in a group of three or four students. Write a produce shopping guide. This shopping guide will help people shop for produce. Follow these steps:*

1. As a group, choose five fruits and vegetables to research. Check with other groups to avoid repeating the same fruits and vegetables.

   _____

   _____

   _____

   _____

   _____

2. Together, buy two of each of your fruits and vegetables—one that is organic and one that is regular. You may have to go to two different stores. Be sure to write down the cost of each piece (by the piece or by the pound). Bring all ten pieces of produce to class.

3. With your group, study your produce. Compare the organic produce with the regular produce. Look at the colors and sizes. Then touch them. Smell them. Taste them. (Remember to wash them first.) Discuss these questions for each of the five kinds of produce:

   a. Can you tell the difference between the organic and the regular produce?

   b. Do they look the same? (color, size)

   c. Do they feel the same? (softness, hardness)

   d. Do they smell the same?

   e. Do they taste the same?

   f. Do they cost the same?

4. Complete an information sheet like the following for each of the five kinds of produce you researched. Fill in the price for the organic and regular produce. For each of the other categories (color, size, feel, smell, and taste), check (✓) **organic** or **regular**—the one that is better in this category. Then write a short recommendation. For this kind of produce, do you think people should buy organic, regular, or either one?

**KIND OF PRODUCE:** _____

|  | Organic | Regular |
|---|---|---|
| **Price** | _____ | _____ |
| **Color** | ☐ | ☐ |
| **Size** | ☐ | ☐ |
| **Feel** | ☐ | ☐ |
| **Smell** | ☐ | ☐ |
| **Taste** | ☐ | ☐ |

**Recommendation:** _____

_____

_____

5. Put all the charts together to make a produce shopping guide.

For step-by-step practice in the writing process, see the *Writing Activity Book, Basic/Low Intermediate, Second Edition,* Unit 7.

| | |
|---|---|
| Assignment: | Writing a Restaurant Review |
| Prewriting: | Clustering |
| Organizing: | Writing for Your Audience |
| Revising: | Choosing Descriptive Adjectives |
| | Using Count and Non-Count Nouns |
| Editing: | Correcting Run-on Sentences |

For Unit 7 Internet activities, visit the NorthStar Companion Website at http://www.longman.com/northstar.

# "I'll take the train, thanks."

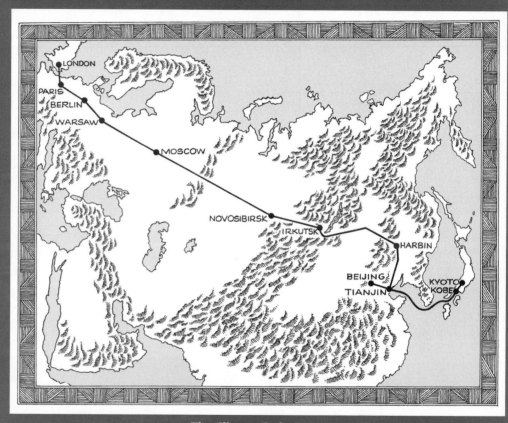

**The Climate Train Route**

# 1 Focus on the Topic

## A PREDICTING

Look at the map. It shows a route that some travelers took in 1997 to go from London, England, to Kyoto, Japan. Discuss these questions with the class.

1. How do you think these people traveled?

2. Why do you think they traveled this way?

3. Why do you think they were going to Kyoto?

## B   SHARING INFORMATION

*Imagine that you live in Madrid, Spain, and you have a two-week vacation. You want to go to Florence, Italy. Florence is about 1,000 miles from Madrid. How will you travel?*

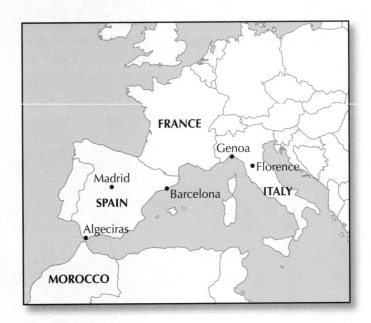

*Look at different ways of traveling between Madrid and Florence. Number your choices (**1** for your first choice, **2** for your second choice, and so on), and write reasons for your decision. Discuss your answers with a partner.*

| Way to Travel | Number | Reason(s) |
|---|---|---|
| **Plane** | | |
| **Train** | | |
| **Car** | | |
| **Bicycle** | | |
| **Car + Boat** | | |

## C   PREPARING TO READ

### BACKGROUND

*Read the following text about climate change. New vocabulary words are explained in parentheses ( ).*

Most scientists all over the world agree that one of the biggest problems in the world right now is the problem of climate (weather) change. All of the pollution (dirty air that comes from cars, planes, factories) is making the world's climate warmer. This warmer weather is melting the ice at the North and South Poles, and the water from the melting ice makes the oceans rise. Also, when weather changes, plants and animals have to change, too. The only way to stop this climate change is to make less pollution.

The United Nations had the first international conference (meeting), about the problem of pollution and climate in 1996. There have been six conferences since then. Each conference tries to get all of the countries of the world to agree on how to make less pollution. Each conference has had some success, but there is still a lot of work to do.

*Now answer the following questions. Discuss your answers in a small group.*

1. What is happening to the world's climate?

2. What causes climate change?

3. Why does the United Nations have international conferences about pollution and climate change?

### VOCABULARY FOR COMPREHENSION

*Read the text below and pay attention to the underlined words.*

Jamal and Hamid are going on vacation to Spain. They live on the north <u>coast</u> of Morocco, so they are going to take the <u>ferry</u> across the water to Algeciras, Spain. Getting the tourist <u>visas</u> was <u>complicated</u>. They had to fill out many forms and get pictures taken. They finally got the visas last week, so they shouldn't have any problems at the <u>border</u>. Hamid <u>arranged</u> to stay with his Spanish friend, Gerardo, while they are there. Jamal and Hamid wanted to take an early ferry, but Gerardo asked them to check the ferry <u>schedule</u> and take a later one so that he could meet them at the <u>dock</u>. Gerardo works with teenage boys. He never leaves work early, because he thinks that it is important to <u>set an example</u> for the boys.

Gerardo has a week off while Hamid and Jamal are visiting. Last year, Gerardo stayed with Hamid in Morocco. He really <u>appreciated</u> Hamid's kindness, so he is excited to show his friends around southern Spain this week.

*Now write the words next to their definitions.*

| appreciate | border | complicated | ferry | set an example |
| arrange | coast | dock | schedule | visa |

1. _____: the line between two countries

2. _____: place where people get on and off a boat

3. _____: an official mark put on your passport that gives you permission to enter a country

4. _____: list of times that ferries, trains, buses, etc. leave or arrive at a particular place

5. _____: to organize and plan

6. _____: boat that takes people, and sometimes cars, back and forth between two places

7. _____: not simple; with lots of details

8. _____: to do something that you hope other people will copy

9. _____: where the land meets the sea

10. _____: to understand and know something is important

# 2 Focus on Reading

## A    READING ONE: *The Climate Train*

*Look at the map on page 143 and put a check (✓) next to the kinds of transportation that you think the Climate Train travelers used.*

_____ train    _____ airplane    _____ car    _____ walking    _____ bus

_____ boat    _____ truck    _____ horse    _____ bicycle    _____ motorcycle

*Now read the whole article. Were your guesses correct?*

# The Climate Train

By Jackson Karl

1   In December 1997, thousands of scientists and other interested people traveled to Kyoto for an international conference on climate and pollution. Months before the conference, most of these people began making airplane reservations. But one English scientist named Ben Matthews thought that flying to Kyoto didn't seem right. He thought, "Airplanes make a lot of pollution . . . Is it right to travel on airplanes so that we can talk about ways to make less pollution?" Ben believes that in order to make less pollution, all people—even scientists—need to change the way they live. He decided to set an example.

2   He began to plan a trip to Kyoto that made less pollution than an airplane trip. Other people soon joined him until there were 36 people from 14 countries ready to travel by land and sea to Kyoto. The group called itself "the Climate Train."

3   Planning the Climate Train trip was very complicated. Ben and his fellow travelers had to carefully choose a route, check schedules, buy tickets, and arrange overnight stays in some towns—all in many different languages. They also had to get visas for every country that they traveled through, even if they didn't stop there.

4   The Climate Train group left England on November 7. They didn't have all of the visas or tickets, but they had to get to the Kyoto conference by December 1. They took many different trains through Brussels, Berlin, Moscow, and Beijing to Tianjin on the coast of China.

5   While they were traveling, the Climate Train group worked a lot, but they also found some time to have fun. They especially liked talking to other travelers and listening to Russian pop music. One evening, some of the other travelers even started dancing on the tables of the restaurant car!

6   At the Chinese border, the border guard took away the group's fresh fruit and vegetables. But they didn't mind, because they were excited to try the different kinds of Chinese food for sale at the border. The problem was that they didn't know what they were buying because almost none of them spoke Chinese. Most of the food came in colorful packages and was delicious, but one of the packages a traveler bought was full of chicken feet. Even the Chinese travelers weren't interested in tasting those!

7   From Tianjin, they traveled for two nights on a ferry to Kobe, Japan. Most of the group got seasick, so they couldn't work or have fun. But they all felt better when they saw the large group of journalists waiting for them at the dock in Kobe.

8   After talking with the journalists, a few Climate Train travelers took the train to Kyoto, and the rest went there on bicycles.

It took the bicyclists three days to ride the 80 kilometers from Kobe to Kyoto.

9    At the conference, the Climate Train travelers talked with many people about their journey.[1] They were glad they had traveled over land and sea, because they showed the world that people can travel long distances in ways that make much less pollution than flying.

10    The long journey helped the travelers appreciate the reasons for the Kyoto Conference. They had to stop at many borders, but they realized that pollution does not stop at borders. They saw so much beautiful countryside on their trip. It made them sad to think that the countryside will change if the climate continues to change.

11    The people on the Climate Train hope that other travelers will follow their example. The five-week round-trip[2] journey was difficult, but only because so few people travel this way. Says Ben, "If more people travel this way, it will become easier." Perhaps there will come a day when buying a round-trip train/ferry ticket from London to Kyoto will be as easy as buying an airplane ticket. If more travelers choose trains and ferries, the world's climate will also be healthier, and travelers will appreciate the world's different countries and cultures more.

[1] *journey:* a long distance trip.
[2] *round trip:* a trip to a place and back again.

*Source:* Based on information on http://www.chooseclimate.org/climatetrain/.

## READING FOR MAIN IDEAS

*Read the questions. Circle the best answer for each question.*

1. What is the main reason that the Climate Train group traveled by land?
   a. to make less pollution
   b. to save money
   c. to learn about other cultures

2. Was the Climate Train group happy that they chose to travel by land?
   a. No. They will take a plane next time.
   b. Yes. They were happy, though it was sometimes difficult.
   c. Yes. They were happy because it was an easy way to travel.

3. What is the most important thing the Climate Train group learned to appreciate on their journey?
   a. The international conference on climate and pollution is very important.
   b. Russian trains have fun restaurant cars.
   c. It's important to understand the language so that you know what kind of food you are buying.

4. What do the Climate Train travelers hope that other people will do?
   a. spend more time at borders
   b. travel by land and sea instead of by air
   c. go to more international climate conferences

## READING FOR DETAILS

*The statements below are false. Correct them. Change a word or phrase in each statement to make it true.*

1. The Climate Train was a ~~train in Russia~~. *group of people*

2. The people on the Climate Train were from England.

3. The travelers needed visas to get on the trains.

4. The group left England after they got all of their tickets and visas.

5. The Climate Train travelers liked working with the other people on the train.

6. The travelers didn't like Chinese fruit and vegetables.

7. Several of the travelers got sick in Japan.

8. All of the travelers rode bicycles from Kobe to Kyoto.

9. The travelers understood that climate does not stop at borders.

10. They think that if more people travel by train and ferry, it will become faster.

## REACTING TO THE READING

**1** *Read each statement. Check (✓) **True, False**, or **?** (if the information isn't in Reading One). Look at the paragraphs indicated in parentheses to help you.*

|  | True | False | ? |
|---|:---:|:---:|:---:|
| 1. Ben Matthews believes that airplanes make more pollution than trains and ferries. (*paragraph 1*) | ❑ | ❑ | ❑ |
| 2. Most people who went to the Kyoto Conference traveled on the Climate Train. (*paragraph 1*) | ❑ | ❑ | ❑ |
| 3. Ben Matthews never travels by airplane. (*paragraphs 1, 2*) | ❑ | ❑ | ❑ |
| 4. The Climate Train travelers enjoyed meeting other travelers on the trains. (*paragraphs 5, 6*) | ☑ | ❑ | ❑ |
| 5. The Climate Train travelers didn't like talking to journalists about their trip. (*paragraphs 7, 8, 9*) | ❑ | ❑ | ❑ |
| 6. By traveling slowly, the Climate Train travelers understood even more why the conference was very important. (*paragraph 10*) | ❑ | ❑ | ❑ |
| 7. The Climate Train travelers helped to make a good agreement at the Kyoto Conference. (*paragraphs 10, 11*) | ❑ | ❑ | ❑ |

**2** *Read this quote and answer the following questions. Then discuss your answers in a small group.*

Some people who don't agree with Ben Matthews say, "You aren't making less pollution. Whether you buy a ticket or not, the plane still goes and makes the same amount of pollution with or without you. One person doesn't make a difference."

**1.** What do you think Ben says to these people who do not agree with him?

_____

_____

_____

**2.** Do you agree with the quote above, or with Ben? Explain your answer.

_____

_____

_____

**B** **READING TWO:** *On the Road with John Madden*

*Read the following article about a well-known figure in the world of American football who travels a lot.*

## ON THE ROAD WITH
# JOHN MADDEN

### BY STEVE MAC

1    Mention John Madden to most Americans, and smiles come to their faces. They think of the jolly football TV announcer who also appears in many commercials. John Madden was also the coach[1] for the Oakland Raiders football team for ten years.

2    As a football announcer, John Madden has to travel about 80,000 miles (130,000 km) during each football season. A football game in Philadelphia on Monday, a party in Detroit on Tuesday, filming a TV commercial in Los Angeles on Saturday . . . He might be the perfect example of a jet setter[2], except for one thing: He never travels by plane.

[1] *coach:* a sports teacher for people who compete in that sport.
[2] *jet setter:* a person who travels all over the world a lot, usually by plane (jet).

3   John Madden is one of 25 million people in the United States who are afraid of flying. These people spend millions of dollars every year trying to cure their fear of flying. They go to classes, they see psychologists, and they take medications to help them with their fear, because they think that they can't live normal lives if they can't fly.

*John Madden commentating a football game.*

4   John Madden decided not to try to cure his fear of flying; he decided to work with it. While he was coaching the Oakland Raiders, he used to travel by train. Then he bought a motor home and decided that was a better way to travel. He has owned several motor homes over the last few years. The last one he bought is 45 feet long with a lounge, office, small kitchen, and 1½ bathrooms. He has three TVs and a full-size refrigerator.

5   Madden travels with several people who drive for him so that he can be on the road 24 hours a day if he needs to be. He probably travels more comfortably than even first-class air passengers. His fear of flying doesn't seem to get in his way[3] at all. He is a great example for people who are afraid of flying. Let's just hope that they don't all go out and buy motor homes!

---

[3] *get in one's way:* to prevent somebody from doing something.

*Now answer the following questions.*

**1.** How does John Madden travel?

_____

**2.** Why does he choose to travel this way?

_____

**3.** How did he travel before?

_____

**4.** Look at the last sentence of the text. What will happen if everyone who is afraid of flying goes out and buys a motor home?

_____

## C  LINKING READINGS ONE AND TWO

The Climate Train travelers and John Madden both prefer not to travel by air.
When they choose a different way to travel, what is the most important thing
to them?

*Fill in the lists below. You can use some of the items in the box (you don't need to include
all of them). Then compare your lists with your partner's.*

| | |
|---|---|
| being able to work while traveling | not feeling afraid |
| comfort | scenery |
| cost | setting an example |
| learning about other places | speed |
| low pollution | traveling with others |

**Climate Train travelers**
Very important things while traveling:
_____
_____

Somewhat important:
_____
_____

Not so important:
_____
_____

**John Madden**
Very important things while traveling:
_____
_____

Somewhat important:
_____
_____

Not so important:
_____
_____

# 3 Focus on Vocabulary

**1** *Read the following statements. Each statement could be said by one of the travelers in
the chart on page 153. Who is most likely to say what? Write the number of each
statement under the correct traveler.*

1. "I'm going from Chicago to Frankfurt. This is the least complicated way
to go."

2. "I like to make my own schedule, and I like driving. That's why I travel
this way."

3. "I usually arrange my vacations so that I can get lots of exercise while traveling."

4. "We are only stopping for 30 minutes in France on the way to Italy, so I don't need a visa."

5. "I think I can finally see the coast. It will be good to get on land again."

6. "All of the passengers had to get off at the border, then we all got back on and continued our trip."

7. "My family came to the dock to say good-bye to me."

8. "I appreciate the older, slower, relaxed ways of traveling overland."

| Train passenger | Airplane passenger | Motor home owner | Bicycle rider | Ferry passenger |
|---|---|---|---|---|
|  | 1 |  |  |  |

**2** *Complete the sentences below with the correct words from the box.*

| | | | | |
|---|---|---|---|---|
| appreciates | border | complicated | ferry | set a bad example |
| arrange | coast | dock | schedule | visa |

1. Linette is afraid of going over bridges, so she drives to the _____ and takes the _____ into the city every day.

2. Traveling to the small town in the Sahara Desert to visit my sister was very _____ and uncomfortable. My daughter complained a lot, but so did I. I guess I _____ for her.

3. I need to check the bus _____. Then we can _____ the trip to New Orleans.

4. Make sure that you have your passport and your _____. They will check both at the _____.

5. Nicole _____ the beach and warm weather. That's why she lives on the _____.

**3** *Read the following information.*

Ben is talking with a travel agent.  He wants to travel from London to Warsaw for another important conference.  He does not want to take a plane for the same reasons he didn't take a plane to Kyoto in 1997.

*Now complete the conversation between Ben and his travel agent.  Use at least eight of the words from the box.*

| | | | |
|---|---|---|---|
| afraid of flying | coast | journey | schedule |
| appreciate something | complicated | pollution | set an example |
| arrange | dock | ride a bicycle | visa |
| border | ferry | round trip | |

BEN:     Hello. I need some information about going to Warsaw from England. I don't want to fly.

AGENT:  Oh that's going to be complicated and expensive . . . You know, there are medications to help with the fear of flying . . .

BEN:     _____

AGENT:  _____

BEN:     _____

AGENT:  _____

BEN:     _____

AGENT:  _____

BEN:     _____

# 4 Focus on Writing

## A  STYLE:  Connecting Sentences with *And* and *But*

**1** *Read the following summary of the movie,* French Kiss.

# French Kiss

The movie, *French Kiss*, tells the story of an American woman named Kate. Kate was afraid of flying, but her fear wasn't a big problem for her. She could lead a normal life. She didn't have to travel for work, and her friends and family lived nearby.

One day, her fiancé asked her to fly with him to Paris where he had to attend a medical conference. She signed up for a fear of flying class, but she failed it. Poor Kate just couldn't get on the airplane, so she stayed home.

When Kate heard that her fiancé found another girlfriend in Paris, she was really angry. "Could you explain this to me?" she asked him over the phone right before he hung up.

She decided that she had to go to Paris to find him. Kate was very nervous when she got on the plane, but she knew she had to go. Then Luc sat down in the seat next to her and introduced himself. Luc told Kate that she couldn't say his name correctly, and Kate told Luc that he was rude. Soon, they were arguing, and Kate was so angry that she forgot that she was nervous about flying.

By the end of the movie, Luc and Kate fall in love. Now they live in France, and they can travel wherever they want. Kate is no longer afraid of flying, but she still can't speak French very well.

*Now reread the summary and circle all of the* ands *and* buts. *What is the difference between **and** and **but?***

## Connecting Sentences with *And* and *But*

**1.** The connector word *and* connects sentences that have **similar** ideas or sentences that you expect to find together.

- She didn't have to travel for work, **and** her friends and family lived nearby.
  *(reason not to fly)*                              *(reason not to fly)*

**2.** The connector word *but* connects sentences that have **contrasting** ideas or sentences that you don't expect to find together.

- She signed up for a fear of flying class, **but** she failed it.
  *(most people pass the class)*

**3.** When you connect two sentences with *and* or *but*, use a comma (**,**) between the ideas.

- Kate was afraid of flying, **but** her fear wasn't a big problem for her.

**4.** When the subject of both sentences is the same, use a pronoun as the subject in the second sentence.

- Kate was very nervous when she got on the plane, **but** ~~Kate~~ *she* knew she had to go.

**2** *Complete the sentences with the correct connector word (**and** or **but**). Add the correct punctuation.*

1. Luc was really rude __, but__ Kate liked him when she got to know him.

2. Kate's fiancé loved Kate _____ he loved his new girlfriend even more.

3. Kate read books about the fear of flying _____ she took classes to help cure her fear.

4. Kate didn't like Luc at first because he was rude _____ he drank too much alcohol.

5. Kate hated flying _____ she needed to go to Paris to find her fiancé.

6. Luc tried to help Kate get her fiancé back _____ she didn't want him back in the end.

7. Kate's French was bad _____ Luc's English was worse.

8. Kate and Luc fell in love _____ they decided to stay in France.

**3**  *Finish the sentences.  For sentences 5 and 6, write your own sentences using **and** and **but**.*

1. Ben Matthews likes being at conferences, but _____ .

2. John Madden is famous, and _____ .

3. Pollution doesn't stop at borders, but _____ .

4. The Climate Train travelers met very interesting people on their trip, and

_____ .

5. _____

6. _____

---

## B    GRAMMAR: *Can* and *Could*

**1**  *Reread the* French Kiss *summary on page 155, and notice the use of the words **can**, **can't**, **could**, and **couldn't**.  Answer the questions below.*

1. What does *can* mean?

2. What is the difference between *can* and *can't*?

3. What is the difference between *can* and *could*?

### *Can* and *Could*

| | |
|---|---|
| **1.** Use ***can*** to express possibility or ability in the present. | They **can** travel wherever they want. *(They are able to travel wherever they want.)* |
| ***Can't*** is the negative of *can*. | She still **can't** speak French very well. *(She still isn't able to speak French very well.)* |
| **2.** Use ***could*** to express ability or possibility in the past. | She **could** lead a normal life. *(It was possible for her to lead a normal life.)* |
| ***Couldn't*** is the negative of *could*. | Kate just **couldn't** get on the airplane. *(It was not possible for Kate to get on the airplane.)* |

*(continued)*

> **3.** *Can* and *could* are also used to make polite requests.
>
> **Can** I travel with you?
> **Could** you explain this to me?
>
> **4.** Always use the **base form** of the verb with *can, can't, could*, and *couldn't*.
>
> BASE FORM
> He **can** *travel* wherever he wants.
> She **could** *lead* a normal life.

**2** *Complete the text with* **can, can't, could,** *or* **couldn't** *and the base form of the verb. Pay attention to present and past time.*

Twenty years ago, we _____ easily with people in many
      **1.** (not/communicate)
different places. If you needed to arrange a presentation, for example, with

someone who lived in Houston, and you lived in Detroit, you

_____ by telephone, and you _____ notes
   **2.** (talk)                 **3.** (send)
to each other by mail. Or, perhaps you _____ a business trip
           **4.** (take)
to have a meeting with that person. You certainly _____ very
               **5.** (not/work)
quickly, compared with the way things are today.

Today things are very different. There are so many fast ways that we

_____ with people in faraway places. We _____
    **6.** (communicate)                 **7.** (still/talk)
on the phone. With conference calling, we _____ with several
            **8.** (talk)
people at once. The problem with conference calls is that you sometimes

_____ who is talking. So some people use videoconferencing
   **9.** (not/tell)
now so that they _____ and hear who is talking. We
         **10.** (see)
_____ faxes and e-mail if we need to share papers with
  **11.** (also/send)
someone quickly.

So with all of these modern ways to communicate, why _____
               **12.** (we/not/stop)
traveling so much for business? Businesspeople find that even though they

_____ and talk to people in videoconferencing, or have good
  **13.** (see)
discussions on e-mail, you _____ personal contact. There is
        **14.** (not/replace)
no substitute for being there in person.

**3** *Using the words provided, write sentences about how each of the following people can/can't/could/couldn't travel. In number 3, you need to write two of your own sentences.*

1. Alex is afraid of flying. She lives in Florida. Her sister is getting married in New York next month. Alex has ten days off of work to go to New York.

   **a.** (train) *She can go by train.* _____

   **b.** (plane) _____

   **c.** (bicycle) _____

2. Natalie and John are on vacation in Seoul, Korea, with their one-year-old son. They want to go to Tokyo, but there is an airport strike there, so the airport is closed.

   **a.** (ferry) _____

   **b.** (car) _____

   **c.** (plane) _____

3. I was backpacking in the mountains in Switzerland. We were three miles from the nearest road and five miles from the nearest town. I fell down and hurt my knee very badly.

   **a.** (walk) _____

   **b.** *(your own sentence)* _____

   **c.** *(your own sentence)* _____

## C   WRITING TOPICS

*Choose one of the following topics. Write one or two paragraphs. Use some of the vocabulary, style, and grammar that you learned in this unit.*

1. Write about ways that you can make less pollution when you travel. Think about the traveling that you do in your daily life (to school, work, or the store, for example) as well as the traveling that you do for vacations.

2. Write about someone you know who does not like to fly. Why doesn't that person like to fly? How does he or she travel? Can he or she drive? Can he or she travel by boat?

3. Write about a long trip that you took over land and/or sea. Describe the trip. What are some new things that you learned to appreciate on this trip?

4. Today, airplanes can take us almost anywhere in the world in less than 24 hours, but before airplanes, people couldn't travel to a lot of places so easily. Compare traveling before airplanes and travel today.

## D RESEARCH TOPIC

*To be a good travel agent, you have to be able to help people with special needs, like people who do not want to fly. Could you be a good travel agent? To find out, follow these steps:*

1. Work in a small group. Choose a place to travel to that people would usually go to by plane.

2. Research other ways to travel to that place. Each person in the group should find out about one way of getting there.

3. Complete the information sheet below.

TO: _____

FROM: _____

| Way of traveling | Stops or overnight stays | Round-trip cost | Time for one-way journey | Benefits | Problems |
|---|---|---|---|---|---|
| Train | | | | | |
| Bus | | | | | |
| Car | | | | | |
| Bicycle | | | | | |
| Boat | | | | | |
| Ferry | | | | | |
| Train + bus | | | | | |
| Train + ferry | | | | | |
| Car + ferry | | | | | |
| Car + bicycle | | | | | |
| (Add your own) | | | | | |
| (Add your own) | | | | | |

**4.** With your group, write a short report based on the information in your information sheet. If possible, draw a map showing the route(s) of the journey.

**5.** Share your report with another group. Read the other group's report. Then answer these questions:

   **a.** Did the writers use *and* and *but* correctly? Circle any incorrect *and* or *but*.

   **b.** If the writers used *can* or *could*, did they use them correctly? Put a star (★) next to the ones that might be incorrect. Talk it over with the other group.

   **c.** Is there a sentence you do not understand? Underline it. Ask the other group to explain it to you.

**6.** Report to the class. Listen to the other reports. Which group has the best travel agents? Why?

For step-by-step practice in the writing process, see the *Writing Activity Book, Basic/Low Intermediate, Second Edition,* Unit 8.

| | |
|---|---|
| Assignment: | Writing Two Comparison and Contrast Paragraphs |
| Prewriting: | Charting |
| Organizing: | Outlining |
| Revising: | Connecting Ideas with *And* and *But* |
| | Expressing Ability and Possibility with *Can* and *Can't* |
| Editing: | Punctuating Sentences with *And* and *But* |

For Unit 8 Internet activities, visit the NorthStar Companion Website at http://www.longman.com/northstar.

# The Winter Blues

# 1 Focus on the Topic

## A PREDICTING

Look at the picture, and discuss these questions with the class.

1. This woman is not really sick. Why is she still in bed at noon?

2. What ideas do you have about why she might feel the way she does?

3. Read the title of the unit. What do you think it means?

## B    SHARING INFORMATION

*Read the dictionary definitions for* **depressed.** *Then discuss the questions below in a small group.*

**de • pressed** /di′prest/ *adj* **1.** feeling sad and unhappy. **2.** suffering from a medical condition (depression) that makes you so unhappy that you cannot live a normal life.

**1.** How are the two definitions of *depressed* different?

**2.** Someone is depressed in the sense of definition (1). What do you think he or she can do to feel better?

**3.** Someone is depressed in the sense of definition (2). What do you think he or she can do to feel better?

## C    PREPARING TO READ

### BACKGROUND

*Read the information about depression.*

*Depressed* is a word that can cause some confusion and misunderstandings. A student who receives a grade of D on a test might say "Oh, I'm so depressed" when he sees his grade. But then, an hour later, he is playing Frisbee with his friends and laughing. We get so used to hearing people say "I'm depressed" in this casual way that we sometimes forget that *depressed* can also refer to a very serious medical condition.

About 10–20 percent of people suffer from depression (also called *clinical depression*) sometime in their lives. Unlike the student with the D, people who are clinically depressed don't forget about their unhappiness. Their "low feeling" is not a temporary mood. They often find it very difficult to work and concentrate. There are many reasons for depression,[1] and there are many ways to help people who have it. People who think they may be clinically depressed should see their doctors.

*Now read each statement. Decide if it is true or false. Write **T** (true) or **F** (false) next to it.*

_____  **1.** A depressed mood usually goes away easily.

_____  **2.** If someone says "I'm depressed," you should take him or her to the doctor immediately.

_____  **3.** If a person feels depressed for a long time, he or she should probably see a doctor.

_____  **4.** People get clinically depressed because they don't do well in school.

---

[1] In the rest of this unit, the words *depressed* and *depression* refer to clinical depression.

## VOCABULARY FOR COMPREHENSION

**1** *Read the following story about Valerie. Try to guess the meanings of the underlined words.*

Valerie is depressed. She doesn't know what <u>causes</u> her depression. She only knows that she feels very <u>emotional</u> a lot of the time for no good reason. <u>Bright</u> sunny days, parties, and other things that make most people happy don't seem to <u>affect</u> the way she feels. For a long time, Valerie didn't know that she was depressed. She just thought that she was a naturally sad person.

When Valerie was a teenager, her mother often checked her <u>temperature</u> because she thought that Valerie was getting sick. A few times, her mother took her to the doctor and made him check her <u>blood pressure</u>, heart, <u>breathing</u>, and everything else she could think of to make sure that Valerie was OK.

When Valerie got older and she told her doctor about it, she found out that she had many of the <u>symptoms</u> of depression. She usually had very little energy—she sometimes stayed in bed for whole days at a time. She often didn't feel like eating. Also, if she couldn't <u>reach</u> the phone from her bed, she never answered her phone.

Valerie went to see a <u>psychiatrist</u>, who told her that depression is a <u>common</u> problem, one that he sees all the time. He helped her choose the right <u>treatment</u>. She is taking some medicine that helps her feel less depressed. In addition, once a week she has <u>psychotherapy</u> where she talks to someone about herself and her problems.

**2** *Now read about Matthew, Valerie's friend. Matthew is not depressed. He has another problem. Complete the paragraph with words from the box. Four of the words are not used.*

| | | | | |
|---|---|---|---|---|
| affects | bright | emotional | reach | temperature |
| blood pressure | causes | psychiatrist | symptoms | treatments |
| breathing | common | psychotherapy | | |

Matthew doesn't feel well. He went to his doctor yesterday because he wanted some medication to make him feel better.

The doctor gave Matthew a checkup. The doctor took Matthew's

(1) _____: "98.6. That is normal," the doctor said. He also

checked Matthew's (2) _____: "110 over 70. That is fine."

He listened to Matthew's heart and lungs. "Your (3) _____ is

fine, too."

"So what exactly are your (4) _____?" the doctor asked

Matthew.

"Well, I'm always tired. I don't see friends anymore—I don't really have time. My girlfriend left me about a month ago, so I guess I have been having some (5) _____ problems," Matthew explained. "But Doctor, I don't have a lot of time to talk. I need to get back to work. Can't you just give me some medication so that I can feel better?"

"Actually, I want you to make an appointment to see Dr. Oxfeldt. He is a (6) _____. He can help you find the (7) _____ of your sickness and decide if you need medication. How many hours a week do you work, Matthew?"

"Oh, between 60 and 70. But I love my work. I don't think work really (8) _____ how I am feeling. And Doctor, I just don't have time for another appointment this week."

"Matthew, medications aren't always the best (9) _____. You might just need to stop working so much."

# 2 Focus on Reading

## A    READING ONE: *Seasonal Affective Disorder*

The following article is from a family medical guide—a book that people can use to get information about common medical conditions.

*Look at the title of the article and at its section titles. What kind of information do you expect to find in this article? Check (✓) the things you think you will find.*

_____ Information about reasons why people have SAD

_____ Definition of SAD

_____ Names of good doctors to see if you have SAD

_____ Stories about people who have SAD

_____ Information to help you know if you have SAD

_____ Information about what to do if you have SAD

*Now read the whole article. Were your guesses correct?*

# SEASONAL AFFECTIVE DISORDER (SAD)

1    People who have Seasonal Affective Disorder (SAD) get depressed during the fall and winter. SAD seems to be much more common in some places than in others. For example, in the United States, less than 1 percent of the people in Florida, a southern state, have SAD, but 10–30 percent of the people in Alaska, a northern state, have it.

## Symptoms

2    The symptoms of SAD are almost the same as the symptoms of depression. The biggest difference is that depression can happen at any time of year, but SAD happens only during the fall and winter months. SAD happens particularly in the far north and far south, where there is less light in the winter. The most common symptoms include:

- sleeping more than usual
- eating more than usual
- getting fatter or thinner quickly
- not having enough energy
- thinking about death
- not wanting to be with other people

## Causes

3    Doctors aren't exactly sure about what causes SAD, but they are beginning to understand it better. The cause of SAD might be emotional (for example, some people get depressed during the holidays because they miss their families); the cause might also be chemical. Scientists have found that some chemicals in our bodies are affected by bright outdoor light (more than 1,500 lux[1]). Bright light causes our bodies to make more of some chemicals and less of other chemicals. These chemicals affect our breathing, blood pressure, and body temperature.

## Treatments

4    The three most common treatments for SAD are light therapy, psychotherapy, and drug therapy.[2]

*SAD patient undergoing light therapy*

5    Light therapy is becoming the most common treatment for people with SAD. About 60–80 percent of people who have SAD can feel better if bright light reaches their eyes every day. The light should be

---

[1] We use *lux* to measure how bright a light is. A sunny day is about 10,000 lux. A dining room is usually about 100 lux.

[2] If you think you are depressed or have SAD, you should talk to your doctor. Your doctor can tell you about the best treatment for you.

brighter than 2,500 lux, and the person with SAD should be near it for one-half to three hours per day in the morning. To get this light, a person with SAD can take walks outside on bright mornings or sit near a special bright light. The light should reach the eyes, but it should not be too close or it might hurt the eyes. Light therapy is the most natural, cheapest, and easiest treatment for SAD, but some people don't have the time it requires.

6    Psychotherapy with a professional psychiatrist or psychologist is another common treatment for SAD. In psychotherapy, the patient talks about problems that he or she is having that might be causing the depression. Psychotherapy is probably the best treatment for emotional causes of SAD, but it can take a very long time, and it can be very expensive.

7    Certain kinds of drugs, called antidepressants, are also a common treatment for SAD. These drugs affect the chemicals in our brains. They make most people feel less depressed quickly, but many people can't take these drugs because they actually cause other problems, for example, stomach problems and sleeping problems.

NOTE: New research is showing that a different type of SAD can occur in the summer. Summer SAD is much less common than winter SAD. We don't know much about summer SAD yet, but we do know that the symptoms, causes, and treatments are different. For the latest information on summer SAD, ask your doctor. Currently, SAD refers to winter SAD as described above.

## READING FOR MAIN IDEAS

*Circle the best ending for each sentence.*

1. SAD is _____.
   a. feeling sad
   b. suffering from depression in the winter or fall
   c. being very tired all the time

2. The symptoms of SAD are _____.
   a. like the symptoms of depression
   b. different for everyone
   c. like the symptoms of a cold

3. The causes of SAD _____.
   a. are 100 percent emotional
   b. might be emotional or chemical
   c. are unknown

4. Treatments for SAD include _____.
   a. light, psychotherapy, and drugs
   b. sleeping and exercising
   c. losing weight and eating healthier food

## READING FOR DETAILS

*In the chart below, write the three most common treatments for SAD. Then list the advantages and disadvantages of each.*

| TREATMENT | ADVANTAGES | DISADVANTAGES |
|---|---|---|
|  |  |  |
|  |  |  |
|  |  |  |

## REACTING TO THE READING

**1** *Read each statement. Decide if it is true or false. Write **T** (true) or **F** (false) next to it. Then discuss your answers with the class.*

_____ **1.** People in Canada are more likely to have SAD than people in Mexico.

_____ **2.** Scientists have found the cause of SAD.

_____ **3.** If you are eating more than usual, you probably have SAD.

_____ **4.** Light therapy is a common treatment for depression.

_____ **5.** Lighting a lot of candles in the evening could help a person with SAD.

**2** *Answer the following questions. Give your opinions. Then discuss your answers in a small group.*

**1.** Do you think that a lot of people in your town suffer from SAD? Why or why not?

**2.** Which treatment for SAD do you think would be best? Why?

**3.** Do you think that light affects all people or only people who have SAD? How? Give an example to explain your answer.

## B  READING TWO: *A Sad Woman in Alaska*

Alice suffers from depression. She has seen several doctors over the past three years, but none of the doctors has been able to help her. Now she is seeing a new doctor.

*Read about Alice's experiences.*

# A SAD WOMAN IN ALASKA

1    "I hope that you can help me, Dr. Crowder," Alice said. "I realized I was depressed about three years ago, soon after I moved here to Alaska. So I went to a doctor. She gave me some medication, but it made me really sick. Then, I went to another doctor. He gave me a different medication, but it also made me sick. The next doctor told me I shouldn't eat sugar or drink coffee. I felt healthier, but I still felt depressed. Finally, I tried psychotherapy for about six months, but it just didn't seem to help. I don't know what to do anymore. This is driving me crazy!"

2    "Alice, you told me on the phone that your depression is worse in the winter. Is that right?" Dr. Crowder asked.

3    "Yes," Alice answered. "But isn't that normal? I mean, in the spring and summer it's really beautiful outside and there's lots to do . . ."

4    "Well, it's normal to feel happy when the sun is out and the days are warm, but it's not normal to be so depressed in the winter," the doctor said. "Alice, I think that you have Seasonal Affective Disorder. It's also called SAD. Do you know what that is?"

5    "Yeah, I think so. I'm not sure," Alice said. "It's a kind of winter depression, right?"

6    "You're right, SAD looks like depression," the doctor answered. "But doctors think that the causes may be different than for other kinds of depression," he added.

7    "Different causes?" Alice asked.

8    The doctor explained to Alice that lack of daylight might be the cause of her *winter depression*. He told her that one way to treat SAD is to take a vacation in the wintertime to a sunny place.

9    "Well, that makes sense, Doctor," Alice said. "Since I have a vacation coming up, I'll go to the sunniest place I can find. But what happens when I come home?"

10    "See me when you return," Dr. Crowder said. "If lack of light is the cause of your depression, you should buy some special lights."

11    The first thing Alice did after visiting Dr. Crowder was to check this chart in the newspaper.

### The Anchorage Times
January 1, 2003

| Sunrise and Sunset Around the World for January 1 | | | |
|---|---|---|---|
| Country/City | Sunrise | Sunset | Hours of daylight |
| Argentina/Puerto Santa Cruz | 03:36 | 19:51 | 16:15 |
| Australia/Sydney | 05:47 | 20:10 | 14:23 |
| China /Beijing | 07:36 | 17:31 | 9:55 |
| Egypt/Cairo | 06:51 | 17:06 | 10:15 |
| Japan/Tokyo | 06:51 | 16:35 | 9:44 |
| Korea/Seoul | 06:47 | 16:25 | 9:38 |
| Mexico/Mexico City | 07:10 | 18:10 | 11:00 |
| New Zealand/Christchurch | 04:53 | 20:10 | 15:17 |
| Norway/Rørvik | 10:06 | 14:02 | 3:56 |
| Russia/Moscow | 08:56 | 16:12 | 7:16 |
| Singapore | 06:03 | 18:04 | 12:01 |
| Spain/Barcelona | 08:18 | 17:33 | 9:15 |
| South Africa/Cape Town | 07:52 | 17:49 | 9:57 |
| U.S./Anchorage (Alaska) | 10:13 | 15:53 | 5:40 |
| U.S./Orlando (Florida) | 07:18 | 17:40 | 10:22 |
| U.S./Portland (Maine) | 07:15 | 16:15 | 9:00 |

*Now answer the following questions.*

1. Where does Alice live?

2. What kind of SAD treatment does her doctor recommend?

3. Look at the Sunrise and Sunset Chart on page 171. Where do you think Alice should go on vacation to help with her SAD? Give three possibilities.

## C     LINKING READINGS ONE AND TWO

The following people all have symptoms of depression which began last November. It is now February. All of these people should see a doctor.

*Read about each person. Give an opinion about which therapy a doctor might prescribe. Check (✓) the therapy, and give reasons for your opinion. Discuss your answers with a partner.*

| | Light therapy | Other kinds of therapy | Reasons |
|---|---|---|---|
| **Brita** is 32 years old. She lives in Sweden, and she loves to ski in her free time. She is a nurse in a hospital. She used to work 3 P.M.–11 P.M., but last September she started working from 8 A.M.–4 P.M. She used to ski in the mornings, but now she goes in the evenings, on trails with lights. She has never suffered from depression before. | | | |
| **George** is 48 years old and lives in Texas. His wife left him and moved to New York with their three small children in September. George has not been able to go to work several days this winter because he was feeling so depressed. | | | |
| **Elaine** is from Hawaii. She just finished college and moved to Chicago last August to take a wonderful new job. She is making a lot of money, and she is enjoying her job. But the winter has been very difficult for her. She is starting to miss her family and friends. She wasn't able to go home for Christmas because things were too busy at work. Some of her colleagues invite her out on weekends, but she doesn't feel like going. She is wondering if she should move back to Hawaii. | | | |

# 3 Focus on Vocabulary

**1** *Read each pair of sentences. Change one or two words in the second sentence so that the sentences make sense together. Pay attention to the meanings of the underlined words.*

1. Scott has a high <u>temperature</u>. His forehead feels ~~cold~~. *hot*

2. I don't think that the cat is <u>breathing</u>. It is probably ~~alive~~. *dide*

3. Lack of sleep really <u>affects</u> babies' crying. If they don't get enough sleep, babies often ~~laugh~~. *cry*

4. Bob is trying <u>psychotherapy</u> to help him with his problem. He thinks that taking medicine will help. *not help him*

5. I think I have flu <u>symptoms</u>. My stomach hurts, my muscles hurt, and I feel very ~~hungry~~. *sick Replet?*

6. The sun is really <u>bright</u> today. I think I need to ~~take off~~ my sunglasses. *put on*

7. "I'd like to make an appointment with a <u>psychiatrist</u>. I think I am ~~pregnant~~." *depression*

8. Mr. McDonald has high <u>blood pressure</u>. He should eat less salt and try to relax ~~less~~. *more*

9. Sam had to drop out of school because he was having <u>emotional</u> problems. I think that he should talk to a ~~heart~~ doctor. *psychiatrist*

10. Vanessa can't <u>reach</u> the teapot in her cupboard. Her husband, who is ~~shorter~~ than she is, always gets it when she needs it. *taller*

11. A: What are some good <u>treatments</u> for tired muscles?

    B: I would try hot baths, rest, and ~~sneezing~~.

12. Steve and Linda wanted to give their son a <u>common</u> American name. They named him Zbignew.

13. My dentist says that candy <u>causes</u> tooth problems. I guess I need to stop eating apples.

**2** *Complete each paragraph with the correct words from one of the word groups below. These words do not have to be used in the order they are listed.*

> blood pressure—cause—emotional
> breathing—reached
> bright—symptoms—treatment
> common—temperature—temperature—treatment
> psychotherapy—psychiatrist

1. When we get worried, our _____ often goes up.
   _____ problems can _~~temperature~~_ high blood pressure.

2. A normal, healthy person's _~~temperature~~_ is 98.6 F (37° C), but it is
   _____ for a person to have a higher _~~temperature~~_ if he
   or she has a bad cold. A good _~~treatment~~_ is to put cold cloths on
   the person's head.

3. Some of my relatives say that grandfather went crazy after grandmother
   died. But maybe he just needed _____ or some other kind of
   help. There was only one doctor in the town and he wasn't a
   _____, so maybe he didn't know what kind of help my
   grandfather needed.

4. Jean thinks she has SAD because she never wants to go to work on days that
   aren't _____ and sunny. But she doesn't have any other
   _____ of SAD. I think the best _____ for her
   problem is a new job!

5. Jason's grandfather got very sick last night. He stopped _____.
   But the ambulance came right away and they _____ the
   hospital just in time.

**3** *Karen is an American student from Florida who is living in Finland this year. It is December, and Karen is feeling very depressed. Complete the e-mail that she sends to her friend Paula, on page 175. Use at least eight words from the box.*

| | | | | |
|---|---|---|---|---|
| affect | cause | depression | psychiatrist | symptoms |
| blood pressure | chemical | emotional | psychotherapy | temperature |
| breathing | common | medication | reach | treatments |
| bright | depressed | | | |

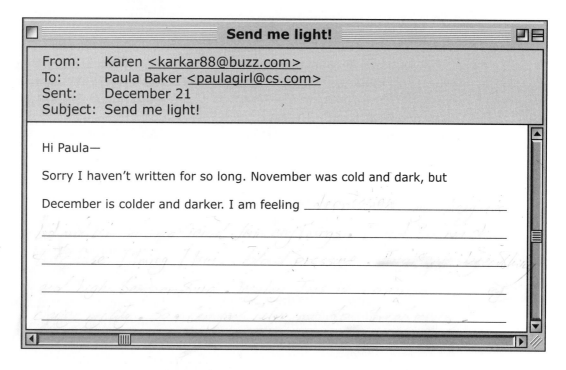

**Send me light!**

From:    Karen <karkar88@buzz.com>
To:      Paula Baker <paulagirl@cs.com>
Sent:    December 21
Subject: Send me light!

Hi Paula—

Sorry I haven't written for so long. November was cold and dark, but

December is colder and darker. I am feeling _____

_____

_____

_____

_____

# 4 Focus on Writing

## A  STYLE: Using Direct Speech

**1** *Read this excerpt from Reading Two. Then answer the questions below.*

"Alice, you told me on the phone that your depression is worse in the winter. Is that right?" Dr. Crowder asked.

"Yes," Alice answered. "But isn't that normal? I mean, in the spring and summer it's really beautiful outside and there's lots to do . . ."

"Well, it's normal to feel happy when the sun is out and the days are warm, but it's not normal to be so depressed in the winter," the doctor said. "Alice, I think that you have Seasonal Affective Disorder. It's also called SAD. Do you know what that is?"

"Yeah, I think so, but I'm not sure," Alice said. "It's a kind of winter depression, right?"

**1.** Which parts of the text are sentences that people actually said?

**2.** How do you know?

## Using Direct Speech

**1.** When you want to report what somebody said, you can use that person's exact words—that is **direct speech.** The exact words that a person said are called **quotes.**

**"Alice, you told me on the phone that your depression is worse in the winter. Is that right?"** Dr. Crowder asked.

**"Yes,"** Alice answered. **"But isn't that normal?"**

**2.** To introduce quotes, you can use **reporting verbs** like *say, add, ask,* or *answer* in the simple past tense.

**a.** Use *say* for quotes which are not questions.

"It's not normal to be so depressed in the winter," the doctor **said.**

**b.** Use *add* when the speaker is adding information to something that he or someone else said just before.

"But doctors think that the causes may be different than for other kinds of depression," he **added.**

**c.** Use *ask* for questions.

"Is that right?" Dr. Crowder **asked.**

**d.** Use *answer* for answers.

"Yes," Alice **answered.**

**3. Punctuation** is important in direct speech.

**a.** Always put **quotation marks** around the quote.

**"**It's not normal to be so depressed in the winter,**"** the doctor said.

**b.** Put a **comma** between a quote and the main subject and verb of the sentence.

"It's not normal to be so depressed in the winter**,**" the doctor said. OR
The doctor said**,** "It's not normal to be so depressed in the winter."

**c.** If the quote is a question, always use a **question mark** at the end of the quote, and before the quotation mark.

"Is that right**?**" Dr. Crowder asked.

**4.** Each time you begin a **new quote** from a different person, you need to start a new paragraph.

"Is that right?" Dr. Crowder asked.
"Yes," Alice answered. "But isn't that normal?"

**2** *Alice was in the store buying a bright light to see if it would help with her SAD. Read the text. Add the missing punctuation.*

The helpful salesperson gave the light to Alice and said OK, here is your 10,000 lux light. Do you know how to use it

Well, my doctor told me a few things Alice answered He said that I should sit near it for two hours every morning

That's right, and you should sit with the light next to your face the salesperson said Remember, you should see the light, but you shouldn't look directly at it he added

**3** *Complete the rest of Alice's conversation with the correct verbs from the box.*

| added | answered | asked | said | said |
|-------|----------|-------|------|------|

"Oh, I won't sit too close. I don't want to hurt my eyes. That light really is bright. But how close should I sit?" Alice **(1)** _____asked_____ .

"About two to four feet away," the salesperson **(2)** _____.

"OK. Thank you very much. You have been really helpful," Alice

**(3)** _____. "I wish I had come here a couple of years ago!" she

**(4)** _____.

"Well I hope the light helps. Feel free to call me if you have any questions," the salesperson **(5)** _____.

**4** *Alice is talking to her brother, Bill, on the phone. Read their conversation. Then, on a separate piece of paper, write a report of this conversation using direct speech.*

ALICE:  So how are you doing, Bill?

BILL:   Oh, not too well. I'm always so tired these days. I can't get up in the morning. I really don't feel like eating much.

ALICE:  I am sorry to hear that, Bill. Have you seen your doctor?

BILL:   No. I think I just don't like the winters here in Montreal.

ALICE:  You know, I thought that was my problem, too. But my doctor just told me I have SAD—Seasonal Affective Disorder.

BILL:   Really?

ALICE:  Yes. Bill, go and ask your doctor about this. Even if you don't have SAD, you should talk to your doctor and see if he can help you out.

BILL:   I guess I should get some help. I will call the doctor tomorrow.

**B** GRAMMAR: *Should* and *Shouldn't*

**1** *Read these sentences from the conversation between Alice and the lighting salesperson on page 177. Notice the use of* **should** *and* **shouldn't**. *Answer the questions below.*

- "He said I should sit near it for two hours every morning."
- "That's right, and you should sit with the light next to your face."
- "Remember, you should see the light, but you shouldn't look directly at it."
- "But how close should I sit?"

1. Why do the speakers use *should* and *shouldn't* in their conversation?

2. What form of the verb do you see with *should* or *shouldn't*?

| **Should** and **Shouldn't** | |
|---|---|
| **1.** Use **should** to give advice or say that something is a good idea. | You **should** sit two to four feet away from this light. *(It's a good idea to sit two to four feet away from the light.)* |
| **2.** Use **shouldn't** to give advice or say that something isn't a good idea. | You **shouldn't** look directly at the light. *(It's a bad idea to look directly at the light.)* |
| **3.** Always use the **base form** of the verb with *should* and *shouldn't*. | BASE FORM<br>You **should** *see* the light.<br>You **shouldn't** *look* directly at it. |

**2** *Complete each statement with* **should** *or* **shouldn't** *and the correct verb from the box.*

| | | | |
|---|---|---|---|
| eat | look | sleep | take |
| exercise | see | stay out | talk |

1. You _____ directly at a bright light.

2. People _____ drugs if their doctors haven't told them to.

3. Jane has all of the symptoms of depression. She _____

   her doctor.

4. My brother is always tired because he goes out almost every night. He

_____ more and he _____ late

every night.

5. Natalie is gaining weight. She _____ more and she

_____ so much ice cream.

6. Jeremy is having serious problems in school, and he's fighting a lot with

other kids. I think he _____ to a psychiatrist.

**3** *Read each statement. Then write a response with* **should** *or* **shouldn't.** *Write at least two sentences with* **should** *and two sentences with* **shouldn't.**

1. I have a terrible headache.

*You should take some aspirin.*

*You shouldn't drink coffee.*

2. I have all of the symptoms of the flu.

_____

_____

3. Dennis was playing football and hurt his back.

_____

_____

4. Richard and his girlfriend fight all of the time.

_____

_____

5. Eddie is losing weight very fast.

_____

_____

6. Catherine is always tired.

_____

_____

## C  WRITING TOPICS

*Choose one of the following topics. Write one or two paragraphs. Use some of the vocabulary, grammar, and style that you learned in this unit.*

1. Do you know anyone who might be depressed? Why do you think he or she is depressed? Did this person say something that made you think he or she is depressed? If this person asks you for advice, what will you tell him or her?

2. Are your moods in the winter different from your moods in the summer? When do you feel saddest? What do you think you should and shouldn't do when you "have the blues" (feel sad)?

3. Write about a time you had a problem and asked for advice from a friend. Write about the discussion you had. What kind of advice did your friend give you? Was it good advice?

## D  RESEARCH TOPIC

*Many depressed people don't know that they can get help. Make a brochure to help other students learn about depression. (See the example on page 181.) Follow these steps:*

1. Work in a small group. To get information for your brochure, go to a local health clinic, public health agency, student health center, or library. If you think that SAD is common in your community, include information about SAD. Take notes.

2. Write your brochure. In this brochure, you should answer the following questions:

   • What is depression?

   • How do I know if I might have it? (What are the symptoms?)

   • What should I do if I think I am depressed?

3. Share your brochure with another group. Read the other group's brochure. Then answer these questions:

   a. Did the writers use *should* and *shouldn't* correctly? Circle the ones that might be incorrect. Talk it over with the other group.

   b. If the writers used direct speech, did they use it correctly? Underline what seems incorrect to you. Discuss with the other group.

   c. Is there a sentence you do not understand? Underline it. Ask the other group to explain it to you.

4. Make sure that your teacher reads your brochure before you give it to anyone else to read. Remember, depression is a very serious illness, so it is important to give correct information.

5. Share your brochure with the class.

What is depression?

*(Write your answer to the question here.)*

**How do I know if I might have it?**

*(Write your answer to the question here.)*

**What should I do if I think I am depressed?**

*(Write your answer to the question here.)*

---

 For step-by-step practice in the writing process, see the *Writing Activity Book, Basic/Low Intermediate, Second Edition,* Unit 9.

| | |
|---|---|
| Assignment: | Writing an Advertisement |
| Prewriting: | Describing Pictures |
| Organizing: | Describing a Process |
| Revising: | Adding Descriptive Details Using Nouns and Adjectives |
| | Using *Should* and *Shouldn't* for Advice |
| Editing: | Punctuating Direct Speech |

 For Unit 9 Internet activities, visit the NorthStar Companion Website at http://www.longman.com/northstar.

# Endangered Cultures

# **1** Focus on the Topic

## A PREDICTING

Look at the pictures, and discuss these questions with the class.

1. These two people are from the same country: Malaysia. Why do you think they look so different from each other? What are the differences?

2. Which person is part of an endangered culture? Explain.

## B    SHARING INFORMATION

Indigenous people are people whose families and cultures have been in one place for a very long time. Many indigenous cultures no longer exist. They are extinct. Almost all indigenous cultures today are endangered. In North America, there are many groups of indigenous people (often called Indians or Native Americans)—for example, the Hopi, the Navajo, and the Shoshone.

*Discuss the following questions in a small group.*

1. What indigenous cultures do you know about?

2. What do you know about them?

3. What is their situation like today?

## C    PREPARING TO READ

### BACKGROUND

The map below shows where most indigenous cultures are found today. There are about 5,000 indigenous cultures in the world today; the map lists a few of them.

*Study the map, and answer the questions on page 185 with a partner.*

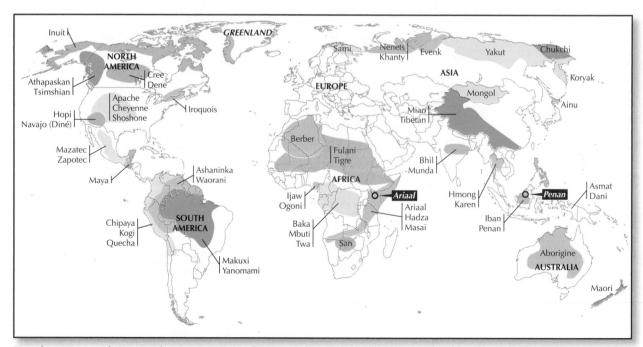

Based on National Geographic map, *National Geographic,* August 1999.

1. Where are there large groups of indigenous people?

2. Look at the coasts (places where the land meets the sea) of North America and Australia. Are there any indigenous cultures there? Who lives there?

3. Are there indigenous people in Europe today? What do you think happened to the indigenous people of Europe?

## VOCABULARY FOR COMPREHENSION

*Match each statement below with the related sentence from the box.*

> a. These cultures have <u>roots</u> in European culture.
>
> b. It is <u>unique</u>.
>
> c. Nobody <u>survived</u>.
>
> d. Now there is a <u>dam</u> on the river.
>
> e. This is the wrong <u>environment</u> for it.
>
> f. She <u>adapted</u>.
>
> g. His <u>ancestors</u> are probably Greek.
>
> h. They are <u>nomadic</u>.
>
> i. He needs to <u>destroy</u> the old one.
>
> j. It is <u>mainstream</u> now.
>
> k. These leaders are <u>holy</u> men or women.

___f___ 1. At first, the food in Kenya made Alex sick, and the weather was too hot. But after a month, she was comfortable.

_____ 2. John got a new credit card in the mail.

_____ 3. I know that Scott grew up in Washington, and so did his parents. But his last name is Tsekaris.

_____ 4. I tried to grow corn in my garden, but it didn't grow very big.

_____ 5. Many U.S. and Canadian traditions are similar to European traditions.

_____ 6. That handmade table is beautiful. I've never seen anything like it.

_____ 7. The airplane crash was awful.

_____ 8. The Penan are a group of people in Malaysia who live in the forest. They don't live in one place; they move around a lot.

_____ 9. Most religions have religious leaders to communicate with God.

_____ 10. At first, only a few people sang and listened to rap music, but now you can hear rap on radio stations all over the world.

_____ 11. When I was a child, I used to play in the river in this valley. Now there is a huge lake where the river used to be.

# 2 Focus on Reading

*Before you read, look at the title of the article. What do you think is the answer to the question in the title?*

# WILL INDIGENOUS CULTURES SURVIVE?

**By Alex Knight**

1    In northern Colombia, a four-year-old Kogi Indian is carried high into the Sierra Nevada mountains. He will live in a small dark house for 18 years while he learns to be a holy man. In the Amazon, a Waorani hunter finds animals by following their smell. A Mazatec farmer in Mexico sends messages to other Mazatec by whistling[1] across the wide valleys of his mountain homeland.

2    Stories about such people show us that there are many different ways of understanding the world and living life. The way we live is just one way.

3    About 300 million people, or 5 percent of the world's population, are members of indigenous cultures. These cultures have deep roots in their histories, languages, and the places they live in. Sadly, their unique ways of living are disappearing because of the fast changes that are happening all around them.

4    Change is an important part of any living culture. In order to survive, a culture must adapt to some changes in its environment.

Unfortunately, the changes that are happening today are so big and so fast that most indigenous cultures simply cannot adapt to them. For example, in Brazil, a gold rush[2] brought sickness to the Yanomami ten years ago. Now one-quarter of them are dead. In Nigeria, the Ogoni homeland near the Niger River is full of poisons from oil companies. Now the Ogoni can no longer grow food there. And in India, over 250,000 indigenous people have to leave their homes in the Narmada River valley, because the government wants to build several dams on the Narmada River.

5    A few of the people from these cultures may survive, but they will have to move away from the lands of their ancestors, often to poor areas outside of large cities. They will have to learn a new way of living and thinking. Their children will know little about the culture they came from.

6    All over the world, indigenous people are fighting to keep their cultures. They are fighting against powerful governments who

---

[1] *whistling*: making a high or musical sound by blowing through one's lips.
[2] *gold rush*: a time when many people move to one area to look for gold.

want them to become part of the mainstream culture, or against oil and logging companies who want their land.

7    The Ariaal are an example of an indigenous nomadic group in Kenya that has been fighting for years. So far, their culture is surviving. The Ariaal understand that some changes may help them, but that other changes may destroy their way of life. The Ariaal are trying to stop the things that will hurt their culture, but accept the helpful parts of the modern world. For example, the Kenyan government wants the Ariaal to move to villages, because it wants the Ariaal and other indigenous people to become more modern. The Ariaal know that if they move to villages, their nomadic way of life will disappear immediately. So they aren't settling in villages. But some Ariaal are starting to send their children to Kenyan schools. These Ariaal have decided that schools are modern things that can help their culture survive.

8    There are no easy ways to save indigenous cultures, but one thing is certain: If the last indigenous cultures are going to survive, they must adapt, and they must choose how they will adapt, as the Ariaal are trying to do. The big question is: Will the rest of the world let them?

Based on information in Wade Davis, "The issue is whether ancient cultures will be able to change on their own terms," *National Geographic*, August 1999.

## READING FOR MAIN IDEAS

*Circle the phrase that best completes each statement.*

1. All the cultures of the world are _____.
   a. similar to each other
   b. very different from each other

2. Indigenous cultures are disappearing because _____.
   a. big changes are happening too fast
   b. their governments don't want them to adapt to the modern world

3. Indigenous cultures are fighting against _____ to keep their cultures.
   a. governments and big businesses
   b. other indigenous cultures

4. In order to survive, indigenous cultures must _____.
   a. listen to their governments
   b. decide how to adapt

5. For indigenous cultures to survive, the rest of the world must let them _____.
   a. have schools
   b. choose how to change

## READING FOR DETAILS

*The article gives many examples to support general ideas. List the examples below each statement.*

1. Three examples of the ways indigenous cultures understand the world and live their lives.

    a. *The Kogi Indian child goes to live in a dark house for 18 years.*

    b. *The Waorani hunter in the Amazon follows animals' smells.*

    c. *The Mazatec farmer in Mexico whistles to send messages across the valleys.*

2. Three examples of changes that indigenous cultures cannot adapt to, and their results.

    a. _____ (result: _____)

    b. _____ (result: _____)

    c. _____ (result: _____)

3. One example of an indigenous group that is fighting to keep its culture.

    _____

4. One example of something that will hurt the Ariaal way of life.

    _____

5. One example of something from mainstream Kenyan culture that the Ariaal want.

    _____

## REACTING TO THE READING

**1** *Read each statement. Check (✓) **True** or **False**. For true statements, write the number of the paragraph where you found the information. Then discuss your answers with a partner.*

|  | True | False | Paragraph |
|---|---|---|---|
| 1. Cultures must change in order to survive. | ❑ | ❑ | _____ |
| 2. Usually, when a culture dies, all of the people from that culture die. | ❑ | ❑ | _____ |

|  | True | False | Paragraph |
|---|:---:|:---:|:---:|
| 3. It is important for people from indigenous cultures to stay in the place where their ancestors lived. | ❏ | ❏ | _____ |
| 4. Governments often want to hurt people from indigenous cultures. | ❏ | ❏ | _____ |
| 5. The Ariaal won their fight to keep their culture, so it will survive. | ❏ | ❏ | _____ |
| 6. If indigenous people decide how to change on their own, they will survive. | ❏ | ❏ | _____ |

**2** *The article mentions many groups of people who have opinions about what should happen to indigenous cultures. Three individuals from these groups are listed below.*

a government official
an indigenous group leader
the president of a logging company

*Read the following quotes about indigenous people and decide who said each quote. Which one do you agree with most? In a small group, discuss why you chose that quote.*

1. "We are not afraid to change, but we cannot forget everything about our culture and our ancestors."

   Who said it? _____

   Do you agree? _____

2. "We don't want these indigenous people running around like animals. We need to teach them how to be a part of the mainstream culture of our country."

   Who said it? _____

   Do you agree? _____

3. "We are not trying to change cultures. We bought the land from the government, so it is ours. We are giving the people who live there good jobs. They should be happy!"

   Who said it? _____

   Do you agree? _____

## B   READING TWO: *The Penan*

*Read the following journal entry about a visit to an indigenous people from Malaysia: the Penan. (A picture of a Penan nomad is on page 183.)*

June 10

1     I am going back to visit my Penan friends after ten years. The big ships are the first things I notice as I turn my boat to go up the river. They are waiting to get filled up with raw logs from the forests of Penan country.

2     When I arrive at the Penan village of Long Iman, my old friend, Tu'o, greets me warmly. Tu'o was born a nomad, but the Malaysian government convinced Tu'o to move to Long Iman 30 years ago. Since that time, thousands more Penan have moved to villages because their forest home was disappearing. The Penan tried to fight to keep their home in the forest, but the logging companies were too powerful.

3     Long Iman is a sad place. The river there is dirty, and there is mud everywhere. The government promised to build hospitals and schools, but none have been built yet. In the evening, children watch Malaysian news on television, but they don't understand the language. Tu'o says he is sorry about the small amount of food at dinner. "How can you feed your guests in a village? It's not like the forest, where there is plenty of food. In the forest I can give you as much as you want. Here, you just sit and stare at your guests and you can't offer them anything. My house here is well built, and we have mattresses and pillows. But you can't eat a pillow."

4     I am here to find one of the last groups of Penan nomads. There are only about 200 Penan nomads left. The group I am looking for now live in a national park, where the forest is protected. Tu'o says he will take me to them, and we leave the next morning. After three days of traveling, we reach the nomads.

5    Asik, the headman, welcomes us. In the evening, we eat food that the nomads have gathered that day, for example, baskets of fruit, wild mushrooms for soup, delicious greens, and two wild pigs. Sharing is such a part of the Penan's way of life that they do not even have a word for "thank you."

6    When I ask Asik about the villages like Long Iman, he says, "There are no more trees, and all the land is no good. The animals are gone; the river is muddy. Here we sleep on hard logs, but we have plenty to eat."

Based on information in Wade Davis, "The issue is whether ancient cultures will be able to change on their own terms," *National Geographic,* August 1999.

## C    LINKING READINGS ONE AND TWO

The article in Reading One is about indigenous cultures in general. The journal entry in Reading Two is about the Penan, an example of an indigenous group.

*Look at the chart. On the left are general statements from Reading One. Read each statement and decide how the Penan are an example of that general statement. Write the information about the Penan on the right.*

| General Statements from Reading One | How Are the Penan an Example of This? |
|---|---|
| **1.** "These cultures have deep roots in their histories, languages, and the places they live." | *The Penan love the forest because they can get food there. They have always lived there. The Penan in the village are not very happy.* |
| **2.** "Their unique way of life is disappearing because of the fast changes that are happening all around them." | |
| **3.** "A few of the people from these cultures may survive, but they will have to move away from the lands of their ancestors ..." | |
| **4.** "[They are fighting against] oil and logging companies who want their land." | |

# 3 Focus on Vocabulary

**1** *Read each group of sentences. Pay attention to the underlined words. Cross out the sentence that does not make sense.*

1. **a.** You won't read about the Ariaal very much in <u>mainstream</u> U.S. newspapers because they are a small group of people.
   **b.** ~~Nobody in the class knows about that book. It must be very <u>mainstream</u>.~~
   **c.** When <u>mainstream</u> radio stations started playing Britney Spears songs, she ~~became very rich.~~

2. **a.** The people who live in these buildings are <u>nomadic</u>.
   **b.** Many indigenous people used to be <u>nomadic</u>, but most live in villages today.
   **c.** <u>Nomadic</u> people usually move when their animals have eaten all of the food in one area.

3. **a.** American blues music has its <u>roots</u> in African American culture.
   **b.** If you want to kill a weed, you need to kill its <u>roots</u>.
   **c.** Everyone who lives in the United States has modern <u>roots</u>.

4. **a.** My house is really noisy. It is a difficult <u>environment</u> to study in.
   **b.** The Ariaal's <u>environment</u> is very American.
   **c.** Tomatoes grow best in a warm <u>environment</u>.

5. **a.** These cups are all handmade, so each one is <u>unique</u>.
   **b.** McDonald's hamburgers in New York are <u>unique</u>. They are just like the McDonald's hamburgers in Los Angeles.
   **c.** Claire spent a year looking for a wedding dress that was <u>unique</u>.

6. **a.** The backpacking trip through Nepal was tough, but I <u>survived</u>!
   **b.** Today, people who have AIDS can <u>survive</u> for many many years because we have new medicines.
   **c.** I used to <u>survive</u> in Canada, but then I moved.

7. **a.** Several people got headaches on the first day of the trip to the mountains. But after a couple of days, their bodies <u>adapted</u> to being in such a high place.
   **b.** The most difficult thing for Noriko to <u>adapt</u> to when she moved to England was the food.
   **c.** Your hair is fine the way it is. Don't <u>adapt</u> anything.

8. **a.** Muslims all over the world fast (stop eating and drinking) during the <u>holy</u> month of Ramadan.
   **b.** This mountain was a <u>holy</u> place to Native Americans. They talked to God there.
   **c.** Americans only eat <u>holy</u> food.

**2** *Complete the following article with words from the box.*

| | | | | |
|---|---|---|---|---|
| adapted | destroy | mainstream | roots | unique |
| ancestors | environment | nomadic | survived | |

# The Berbers

The Berbers are the indigenous people of North West Africa. They lived there before the Arab conquests of the seventh century. At one time, they were (**1**) _____, but now most of them live in towns and villages. Some Berbers are very light skinned, and some are dark. Nobody is really sure who their (**2**) _____ were, but they probably have (**3**) _____ in both Europe and Africa.

The largest number of Berbers live in Morocco. At one time, the government there wanted to (**4**) _____ Berber culture. But Berber culture (**5**) _____. Berbers (**6**) _____ to the Arab (**7**) _____ they were in. They became Muslim, and most of them learned Arabic.

Many Berbers live (**8**) _____ Moroccan lives now, but most of them still speak Berber, and they return to their villages often so that they don't forget their (**9**) _____ traditions.

**3** You want to interview a person from an indigenous culture. Write a list of questions to ask him or her. Use at least nine of the vocabulary words listed below. Use different types of questions.

| | | | | | |
|---|---|---|---|---|---|
| adapt | companies | government | homeland | modern | roots |
| ancestors | destroy | history | indigenous | nomadic | survive |
| change | environment | holy | mainstream | religion | unique |

1. *Can you tell me about the roots of your culture and language?*

2. _____

3. _____

4. _____

5. _____

6. _____

7. _____

8. _____

9. _____

10. _____

# 4 Focus on Writing

## A    STYLE:  Using Examples

**1** Look at the following two excerpts from the readings. Each excerpt uses examples to make a general statement clearer. In each excerpt, underline the general statement, and circle the examples.

**Excerpt 1**

In the evening, we eat food that the nomads have gathered in that day, for example, baskets of fruit, wild mushrooms for soup, delicious greens, and two wild pigs.

**Excerpt 2**

Unfortunately, the changes that are happening today are so big and so fast, that most indigenous cultures simply cannot adapt to them. For example, in Brazil a gold rush brought sickness to the Yanomami ten years ago. Now one-quarter of them are dead. In Nigeria, the Ogoni homeland near the Niger River is full of poisons from oil companies. Now the Ogoni can no longer grow food there. And in India, over 250,000 indigenous people have to leave their homes in the Narmada River valley, because the government wants to build several dams on the Narmada River.

## Using Examples

There are two ways to use examples when you write.

**1.** If the examples are short, you can include them in the sentence with the general statement.

GENERAL STATEMENT
- In the evening, we eat food that the nomads have gathered that day,
  EXAMPLE 1          EXAMPLE 2                    EXAMPLE 3
  *for example,* baskets of fruit, wild mushrooms for soup, delicious greens,
  EXAMPLE 4
  and two wild pigs.

You can use ***for example*** to introduce the first example.

**2.** If the examples are long, you can put them in separate sentences that follow the sentence with the general statement.

GENERAL STATEMENT
- Unfortunately, the changes that are happening today are so big and so fast

  that most indigenous cultures simply cannot adapt to them. *For example,*
  EXAMPLE 1
  in Brazil a gold rush brought sickness to the Yanomami ten years ago. Now
                              EXAMPLE 2
  one-quarter of them are dead. In Nigeria, the Ogoni homeland near the Niger

  River is full of poisons from oil companies. Now the Ogoni can no longer
                    EXAMPLE 3
  grow food there. And in India, over 250,000 indigenous people have to leave

  their homes in the Narmada River valley because the government wants to

  build several dams on the Narmada River.

You can use ***for example*** plus a comma to introduce the first example (but it is not necessary when your example is a whole sentence).

**2** *Read each group of sentences. Write **GS** next to the general statement and **EX** next to each example.*

1. _____ **a.** Tu'o thinks that there will be a lot of sad changes in Penan culture over the next few years.

   _____ **b.** He thinks that the nomads who are still in the forest will have to move away.

   _____ **c.** He is also afraid that the Penan language will disappear.

2. _____ **a.** For example, he hunts for wild pigs and then sells them to loggers who work in the area, because he knows that his family needs money in the village.

   _____ **b.** Tu'o's son is adapting to Penan life outside of the forest.

   _____ **c.** He also learned to speak Malay.

3. _____ **a.** He is going to meet with the local governor to explain why the forest is so important to the Penan.

   _____ **b.** He is going to a meeting in the capital city in two months with Tu'o's son and three other Penan who speak Malay.

   _____ **c.** Asik is trying to organize his people to try to save the Penan's forest environment.

**3** *Complete the sentences with appropriate examples.*

1. Indigenous cultures are still alive in many places, for example,

   _____, _____, and

   _____.

2. There are several things I don't like about mainstream American culture,

   for example, _____, _____, and

   _____.

3. The Penan in the village lack a lot of things, for example, _____,

   _____, and _____.

4. There are many kinds of fruits and plants that you can eat straight from

   nature, for example, _____, _____,

   and _____.

**4** *Finish the paragraphs. Write at least two more sentences.*

**1.** Many indigenous cultures around the world are disappearing. For example,

_____ .

Also, _____

_____ .

**2.** There are several things you can do to help save indigenous cultures. For

example, you can _____ .

You can also _____

_____ .

And you can _____

_____ .

**B**  **GRAMMAR: Expressing Predictions and Future Plans**

**1** *Read about Asik's trip to the capital city. Underline the verbs that refer to the future.*

Asik is traveling to the capital city in three days to talk with many officials about his people's situation. He is going to bring along three young Penan who speak Malay. They will help him and the people he meets understand each other. He is going to meet the president of the Rainforest Action Network (RAN), and then he is giving a short speech to the Parliament. He is not going to meet with experts from the logging companies. They said, "Are you going to tell us anything new? The land is ours. We bought it, so there is nothing to discuss. Nothing will change." The president of RAN will try to help. The members of Parliament will listen to him politely. But Asik wonders, "Will anything change?" He hopes so, but he is not sure.

*Write an example of each of the three different forms used to talk about the future.*

**1.** _____

**2.** _____

**3.** _____

## Expressing Predictions and Future Plans

There are different ways to talk about the future in English.

**1.** Use *will* + base form of the verb for **predictions.**

They **will listen** to him politely, but they **won't do** anything.

**Will** anything **change?** No, nothing **will change.**

Do not use *will* + base form of the verb for plans made before now.

WRONG: I can't go to the capital with you because I will get married.

**2.** Use *be going to* + base form of the verb for **predictions** or for **plans made before now.**

They **are going to listen** to him politely, but they **are not going to do** anything. *(prediction)*

He **is going to bring** along three young Penan. *(plan made before now)*

**Is** he **going to meet** with the president?

**3.** Use the **present progressive** (*be* + *-ing* form of the verb) for **plans made before now.** Future time is indicated by future time words or by the context.

Asik **is giving** a short speech to the Parliament *next Tuesday.*

When **is** Asik **coming** back?

Do not use the present progressive to make predictions.

WRONG: The Penan are surviving in the future.

**2** *Complete Asik's speech to Parliament. Use a future form of the verbs given. For each blank, two forms are possible; choose one. Use each of the three ways of expressing the future at least once.*

"The government says that it is helping us. The logging companies say

that the Penan people _____ lots of money. But the jobs
        **1.** (earn)

_____ with the forest. When the forest is gone, there
  **2.** (disappear)

_____ any more jobs. Why do we need jobs anyway? My
  **3.** (not be)

grandfather didn't have a job. My father didn't have a job. They lived off

the forest. But there _____ any more forest to live off in a few
                        4. (not be)

years—for anyone.

The people from the government say that they _____ schools
                                              5. (build)

and hospitals for us in the next few years. They say they _____
                                                          6. (help)

us learn to be a part of Malaysian mainstream culture when the schools are

finished. But we don't want to be part of Malaysian mainstream culture. We

_____ the way we are. We _____ from the forest.
  7. (stay)                              8. (not move)

My aunt moved to a government village 20 years ago. She says, "This logging

is like a big tree that has fallen on my chest. I wake up every night and talk

with my husband about the future of my children. I always ask myself, 'When

_____?' "
  9. (it / end)

My elderly grandmother went to live with that aunt a year ago, but she

_____ back to the forest. "I _____ soon," she says.
  10. (come)                              11. (die)

"I _____ in that government village. My spirit _____
   12. (not die)                                              13. (never rest)

there."

**3** *Write six questions about the future of the Penan and other indigenous cultures. For
items 1–3, use the words given. For items 4–6, write your own questions. Make sure you
use appropriate forms.*

**1.** Penan culture / disappear?

_____

**2.** How many / Penan nomads / be alive / in 50 years?

_____

**3.** anyone / speak Penan / in 100 years?

_____

**4.** _____

**5.** _____

**6.** _____

**4** *Work with a partner. Read the questions your partner wrote for Exercise 3. Then write answers to your partner's questions. Make sure you use appropriate forms for talking about the future.*

1. _____
2. _____
3. _____
4. _____
5. _____
6. _____

## C    WRITING TOPICS

*Choose one of the following topics. Write one or two paragraphs. Use some of the vocabulary, style, and grammar that you learned in this unit.*

1. What will the world be like if most indigenous cultures become extinct? Write about your predictions.

2. Is it a good idea to try to save indigenous cultures? Why or why not? Give examples.

3. Some indigenous cultures have become mainstream cultures. Write about one of these cultures, and tell how it adapted. How different is that culture today from the way it was before it became mainstream?

4. Find someone who is from an indigenous culture. Ask him or her about that culture and write about it. Write about how that culture thinks and lives. Be sure to use examples in your writing.

5. What will the mainstream culture in your country be like in 50 years? Write about your predictions.

## D    RESEARCH TOPIC

*Could you be a good reporter on an endangered culture or people? Work in pairs. Follow these steps:*

1. Choose an endangered culture/people from the map on page 184.

2. Go to the Internet or to the library to do research about this group of people. Complete the information sheet on page 201.

**Name of endangered people:** _____

Number of people living:                _____


Environment where they live: _____

_____

_____

Relationship to mainstream culture: _____

_____

_____

Unique ways of living *(give example):* _____

_____

Future predictions for these people *(give examples):* _____

_____

_____

_____

_____

_____

**3.** Write a short report about this endangered culture/people. Expand on the information in your information sheet.

**4.** Share your report with another pair of students. Read the other pair's report. Then answer these questions:

   **a.** Did the writers give examples? Did they do that correctly? Underline any incorrect example. Talk it over with the other pair.

   **b.** Did the writers use future forms correctly? Circle the ones that might be incorrect. Talk it over with the other pair.

   **c.** Is there a sentence you do not understand? Underline it. Ask the other pair to explain it to you.

**5.** Share your report with the class. Listen to the other reports. Which pair has the best reporters?

For step-by-step practice in the writing process, see the *Writing Activity Book, Basic/Low Intermediate, Second Edition,* Unit 10.

Assignment:     Writing Prediction Paragraphs
Prewriting:     Using Information from a Reading
Organizing:     Outlining
Revising:       Writing a Concluding Sentence
                Expressing Future Predictions with *Will* and *Be going to*
Editing:        Correcting Verb Forms

For Unit 10 Internet activities, visit the NorthStar Companion Website at http://www.longman.com/northstar.

# Grammar Book References

| NorthStar: Reading and Writing, Basic/Low Intermediate, Second Edition | Focus on Grammar: A Basic Course for Reference and Practice, Second Edition | Azar's Basic English Grammar, Second Edition |
|---|---|---|
| **Unit 1**<br>Descriptive Adjectives and Possessive Adjectives | **Unit 6**<br>Descriptive Adjectives<br><br>**Unit 10**<br>Possessive Nouns and Possessive Adjectives; Questions with *Whose* | **Chapter 1**<br>Using *Be* and *Have*: 1-6, 1-12<br><br>**Chapter 4**<br>Nouns and Pronouns: 4-2<br><br>**Chapter 8**<br>Nouns, Adjectives and Pronouns: 8-14 |
| **Unit 2**<br>Simple Past Tense | **Unit 4**<br>The Past Tense of *Be*; Past Time Markers<br><br>**Unit 18**<br>Simple Past Tense: Regular Verbs—Affirmative and Negative Statements<br><br>**Unit 19**<br>Simple Past Tense: Irregular Verbs—Affirmative and Negative Statements<br><br>**Unit 20**<br>Simple Past Tense: *Yes/No* and *Wh-* Questions | **Chapter 5**<br>Expressing Past Time |
| **Unit 3**<br>Comparative Forms of Adjectives | **Unit 38**<br>Comparative Form of Adjectives | **Chapter 9**<br>Making Comparisons: 9-3 |
| **Unit 4**<br>*Wh-* Questions in the Simple Present Tense | **Unit 15**<br>Simple Present Tense: *Wh-* Questions | **Chapter 2**<br>Expressing Present Time (1): 2-11, 2-12, 2-13 |

| NorthStar: Reading and Writing, Basic/Low Intermediate, Second Edition | Focus on Grammar: A Basic Course for Reference and Practice, Second Edition | Azar's Basic English Grammar, Second Edition |
|---|---|---|
| **Unit 5**<br>Verbs plus Gerunds and Infinitives | **Unit 27**<br>Verbs plus Nouns, Gerunds, and Infinitives | |
| **Unit 6**<br>Adverbs and Expressions of Frequency | **Unit 25**<br>Present and Present Progressive; *How often . . . ?*; Adverbs and Expressions of Frequency | **Chapter 2**<br>Expressing Present Time (1): 2-2, 2-3 |
| **Unit 7**<br>Count and Non-count Nouns | **Unit 33**<br>Count and Non-count Nouns and Quantifiers | **Chapter 4**<br>Nouns and Pronouns: 4-6, 4-8, 4-9, 4-12 |
| **Unit 8**<br>*Can* and *Could* | **Unit 35**<br>*Can* and *Could* for Ability and Possibility; *May I, Can I,* and *Could I* for Polite Requests | **Chapter 7**<br>Expressing Ability: 7-1, 7-2, 7-4, 7-13, 7-14 |
| **Unit 9**<br>*Should* and *Shouldn't* | **Unit 42**<br>*Should, Shouldn't, Ought to, Had better,* and *Had better not* | **Chapter 10**<br>Expressing Ideas with Verbs: 10-1 |
| **Unit 10**<br>Expressing Predictions and Future Plans | **Unit 32**<br>*Will* for the Future<br><br>**Unit 31**<br>*Be going to* for the Future; Future and Past Time Markers | **Chapter 6**<br>Expressing Future Time: 6-1, 6-5, 6-6 |

# Credits

**Illustration credits:** Dusan Petricic pp. 1, 17, 19, 44, 77, 104, 114; Ron Chironna pp. 37, 51, 54, 57, 58, 59, 60, 103, 123, 139, 163; Lloyd Birmingham pp. 74, 154, 170; Hal Just p. 143

**Photo credits:** Page 8 Wartenberg/Picture Press; **9** *(top)* Rob Lewine Photography/Corbis, *(bottom)* Larry Williams/Corbis; **23** Little Blue Wolf Productions/Corbis; **41** David Young-Wolff/PhotoEdit; **81** Digital Vision/Getty Images; **83** Jon Feingersh/Corbis; **89** Britt Erlanson/Getty Images; **108** Photodisc Collection/Getty Images; **121** Jeff Greenberg/ Omni-Photo Communications, Inc.; **126** Rubberball Productions; **147** Christina Hotz; **151** Photofest; **155** George Etienne/Corbis Sygma; **167** Dan McCoy/Rainbow; **183** *(left)* Robert Holmes/Corbis, *(right)* Eric K. K. Yu/Corbis; **187** Maria Stenzel/ National Geographic Image Collection; **193** J. Du Boisberran.

# Notes

# Notes